# Modernism/Peter Faulkner

ROUTLEDGE

LONDON and NEW YORK

First published 1977
by Methuen & Co. Ltd
Reprinted 1980 and 1985
Reprinted 1990, 1991 by
Routledge
11 New Fetter Lane, London EC4P 4EE
29 West 35th Street, New York, NY 10001
© 1977 Peter Faulkner

Printed in Great Britain by
J. W. Arrowsmith Ltd, Bristol

ISBN 0 415 05145 2

# Contents

# Founder Editor's Preface

The volumes composing the Critical Idiom deal with a wide variety of key terms in our critical vocabulary. The purpose of the series differs from that served by the standard glossaries of literary terms. Many terms are adequately defined for the needs of students by the brief entries in these glossaries, and such terms do not call for attention in the present series. But there are other terms which cannot be made familiar by means of compact definitions. Students need to grow accustomed to them through simple and straightforward but reasonably full discussions. The main purpose of this series is to provide such discussions.

Many critics have borrowed methods and criteria from currently influential bodies of knowledge or belief that have developed without particular reference to literature. In our own century, some of them have drawn on art-history, psychology, or sociology. Others, strong in a comprehensive faith, have looked at literature and literary criticism from a Marxist or a Christian or some other sharply defined point of view. The result has been the importation into literary criticism of terms from the vocabularies of these sciences and creeds. Discussions of such bodies of knowledge and belief in their bearing upon literature and literary criticism form a natural extension of the initial aim of the Critical Idiom.

Because of their diversity of subject-matter, the studies in the series vary considerably in structure. But all authors have tried to give as full illustrative quotation as possible, to make reference whenever appropriate to more than one literature, and to write in such a way as to guide readers towards the short bibliographies in which they have made suggestions for further reading.

*University of Manchester*                                  John D. Jump

# *Acknowledgements*

This book emerges from the teaching of a course on 'Aestheticism and Modernism' at the University of Exeter. I am therefore grateful to Professor Moelwyn Merchant, who encouraged the establishment of the course, and to my colleagues who have contributed sections of this book which have since been edited and reduced: Mr A. Fothergill on Virginia Woolf, and Dr J. Lane, now of the University of Sussex, on Joyce; and to Mr C. H. Page for part of the section on Eliot. The overall responsibility remains mine.

Peter Faulkner

# Introduction

Modernism is a term now frequently used in discussions of twentieth-century literature – indeed, of all forms of twentieth-century art. Like all critical terms, it needs to be used with care and precision if it is to help our understanding of the works it is applied to. Matthew Arnold's injunction about the poetic touchstones suggested in 'The Study of Poetry' remains basic to all attempts at criticism: 'if we have tact and can use them' we begin to be critics; if they use us, we are playing a fruitless game.

It was in the 1920s that the term Modernism began to move from a general sense of sympathy with the modern to a more specific association with experimentation in the arts (though the application to a 'progressive' attitude in religion has been retained). *A Survey of Modernist Poetry* was first published by Laura Riding and Robert Graves in 1927, but the authors tend to use the adjective 'modern' rather than 'modernist' in most of the text of that stimulating book. And it is noticeable that neither I. A. Richards in *The Principles of Literary Criticism* (1924) nor Dr Leavis in *New Bearings in English Poetry* (1932) employed the term Modernism, although both were concerned with 'modern' qualities in poetry, especially that of T. S. Eliot – 'a modern sensibility' as Leavis called him.

This is hardly surprising. Most of our critical terminology which has an historical element is retrospective: the fact that Keats did not call himself a Romantic poet is no reason for us not to employ the critical term. Criticism is in part an attempt to understand past cultures. Critics of recent decades looking back at the earlier part of the century have felt that its works of art have enough in common to justify a single critical description. Hugh Kenner recognized this clearly in his foreword to *Gnomon* in 1958. He also noted that the movement then lacked a name, and proposed to develop Wyndham Lewis' term and call it the Vortex – 'a shaped, controlled and heady circling, centripetal and three-dimensional, around a funnel of calm.' This usage never developed. Graham Hough in *Image and Experience* in 1960 found the same difficulty of terminology:

> The years between 1910 and the Second World War saw a revolution in the literature of the English language as momentous as the Romantic one of a century before ... [But it] has not yet acquired a name.

Hough's suggestion was to extend the term Imagism: 'Imagist ideas are at the centre of the characteristic poetic procedures of our time, and there is a case for giving the word a wider connotation.' Again, this usage has not developed, presumably because the narrower connotation has been found useful. But in the meantime Modernism has come to supply the need. It was not used in 1961 in the volume of *The Pelican Guide to English Literature* discussing the twentieth century; but in *The Sphere History* in 1971 it is freely used, particularly in Bernard Bergonzi's opening essay 'The Coming of Modernism'. This reflects the facts of current critical usage.

The immense variety of works in all the arts to which the term modernist has been applied constitutes a formidable challenge to any attempt at exactness. This study will not attempt to be encyclopedic: it will be concerned with English literary Modernism, the writings above all of T. S. Eliot, Ezra Pound, James Joyce and Virginia Woolf. It will place them in the context of such precursors as Henry James and Yeats, and will consider the influence and contemporary importance of Modernism. That the term is not a vacuous one which includes all twentieth-century writers is suggested by the fact that an important modern writer like Orwell is not thought of as a modernist, and that the relation of D. H. Lawrence to the idea is far from simple. It is hoped that by the end of this study the utility of the term will have been demonstrated and that it will have been given enough substance to make the discussion useful beyond the sphere in which it originates, so that it may cast some light on, say, Picasso or Stravinsky. However, the immediate emphasis is literary, and the intention is not to prescribe but to clarify.

# I

# Development

Modernism is part of the historical process by which the arts have dissociated themselves from nineteenth-century assumptions, which had come in the course of time to seem like dead conventions. These assumptions about literary forms were closely related to a particular relationship between the writer and his readers – on the whole a stable relationship in which the writer could assume a community of attitudes, a shared sense of reality.

The most obvious manifestation of this is the 'realism' of the Victorian novel. Although the novelists were intelligently aware of the varieties of human experience – how otherwise could they have been novelists? – they assumed that they and their readers shared a common reality. On the whole the Victorian novel followed the path entered on by Jane Austen, as suggested by Scott when he praised *Emma* for exemplifying

> the art of copying from nature as she really exists in the common walks of life, and presenting to the reader, instead of the splendid scenes of an imaginary world, a correct and striking representation of that which is daily taking place around him.

This emphasis on common experience is typical of the Victorian novelists – of Thackeray, Trollope, Mrs Gaskell and George Eliot. Thackeray, indeed, complained of Dickens' failure in this respect in a letter to David Masson in 1851: 'I quarrel with his Art in many respects: which I don't think represents Nature duly.' But, while Dickens certainly used sensation, melodrama and coincidence more than his contemporaries, he did not doubt that he was leading his readers into a shared ethical realm where they would recognize the moral truth in the exaggerated or selective representation of life. He had a wider understanding of reality rather than a dismissive attitude to it.

The stress on shared experience explains the habit of direct address in Victorian novels, which modern readers find distressingly coy:

> Ah! *Vanitas Vanitatum!* which of us is happy in this world? Which of us has his desire? or, having, is satisfied? – Come children, let us shut up the box and the puppets, for our play is played out.
>
> (Thackeray, *Vanity Fair*, 1847)

> The author now leaves him [Mr Harding] in the hands of his readers; not as a hero, not as a man to be admired and talked of, not as a man who should be toasted at public dinners and spoken of with conventional absurdity as a perfect divine, but as a good man without guile, believing humbly in the religion which he has striven to teach, and guided by the precepts he has striven to learn.
>
> (Trollope, *Barchester Towers*, 1857)

> But the effect of her [Dorothea's] being on those around her was incalculably diffusive: for the growing good of the world is partly dependent on unhistoric acts; and that things are not so ill with you and me as they might have been, is half owing to the number who lived faithfully a hidden life, and rest in unvisited tombs.
>
> (George Eliot, *Middlemarch*, 1870)

These conclusions to major Victorian novels all appeal directly to their readers in emotional terms, assuming that their experiences of life will be sufficiently like those of the authors to claim assent. Once the novelist senses a likely failure of response in the readers, this kind of ending disappears. With it goes the nineteenth-century consensus.

That consensus, the view that writer and reader share a justified expectation of what literature is and can provide, did not need to be confined to the realistic novel. With the drama it simply took the form of the belief that entertainment was paramount, in burlesque, melodrama, pantomime – or, indeed, Shakespeare. In poetry as in the novel, the expectation was of ethical enlightenment, to be conveyed in a form intelligible to a wide audience. It was because Tennyson was prepared to fulfil these requirements that he came to occupy so prominent a position in the intellectual life of his time. The review of Tennyson's two-volume *Poems* of 1842 by his friend James Spedding reveals the underlying attitude:

> All that is of true and lasting worth in poetry, must have its root in a sound view of human life and the condition of man in the world. Where this is not, the most consummate art can produce nothing which man will long care for – where it is, the rudest will never want an audience.

*In Memoriam* was the poem in which Tennyson managed to fulfil these expectations while at the same time expressing his own deepest perplexities. In his later poems, it sometimes seems as if his sense of public responsibility plays too large a part in determining the nature of what he writes. It was because Tennyson came to accept this 'public' conception of poetry that he was able to fulfil the duties of Poet Laureate with such confidence – and was perhaps the last poet so able to act. In other Victorian poets such as Browning and Hopkins there is a gap between the poetry and the audience's expectations. Browning managed to out-talk his critics, but his poetry became garrulous in the process, while Hopkins did not publish. Tennyson spoke for and to his age, and the *Idylls of the King* themselves were written as his fullest effort to express sound moral teaching in the form of poetry: 'I tried in my *Idylls* to teach men the need of the ideal', he was to say. Few later writers would admit to so directly didactic a purpose, or have such confidence that 'the ideal' was an entity universally recognizable.

The high esteem in which writers like Tennyson and George Eliot were held indicates that Victorian culture accepted literature as socially important, and allowed it to take over some of the functions previously fulfilled by religion. In order to do this, it had to be ethically orientated. But the price of this was a certain lack of force and range in Victorian literature, most notoriously in the treatment of sexual relationships. How little we learn from even the relatively outspoken Dickens about the commonness of prostitution in his society. (There could be no English Balzac or Dostoevsky.) This sense of the limitation imposed on the writer as his part of the social consensus became increasingly irritating, as the period went on, to those more interested in the True and the Beautiful than the Good. On the Continent, especially in France, this had long been the case. Neither Baudelaire nor Flaubert would have fulfilled the bourgeois conception of morality, and both were acutely aware of their alienation. In England the reaction came later with the Pre-Raphaelitism of Rossetti and Swinburne (denounced so vituperatively by Robert Buchanan as 'The Fleshly School of Poetry' in 1871). Aestheticism, as justified by Walter Pater in the Conclusion of *The Renaissance* in 1873, was a direct challenge to the prevailing view that the artist's standing was that of a moral spokesman. For Pater the artist is valuable because he helps to bring about 'a quickened, multiplied consciousness' through his creation of beautiful works. In Oscar Wilde's formulation in 'The Decay of Lying' in 1890 the whole Victorian position is neatly subverted: 'The final revelation is that lying, the telling of beautiful untrue things, is the proper aim of Art'. Thus the moral earnestness of the mid-century was finally dissipated in the extravagances and paradoxes of the Nineties.

Nor was the tradition which passed from the Pre-Raphaelites to the Aesthetes the only one to challenge Victorian orthodoxies. In the theatre, the new drama began to develop, deriving from Ibsen's middle-period plays with their powerful assaults on social convention, like *The Pillars of the Community* (1877) and *A Doll's House* (1879). Bernard Shaw published his three earliest plays in 1898 with the title *Plays Unpleasant*, as a direct attack on the susceptibilities of his audience. As he put it in his Preface: 'I must, however, warn my readers that my attacks are directed against themselves, not against my stage figures.' Far from seeking a consensus, the dramatist is challenging his audience's whole scheme of values. A similar development can be seen in the late nineteenth-century novel. George Moore's attack on the circulating library system in his brilliant pamphlet 'Literature as Nurse, or Circulating Morals' in 1895 marked the end of the easy Victorian agreement about which constituted an acceptable morality. The outraged reception of Hardy's *Jude the Obscure* (1896) shows the shock caused when a novelist tried to alter the focus of the novel. (The Bishop of Wakefield wrote to the *Yorkshire Post* to relate that he had been so disgusted with its insolence and indecency that he threw it on the fire.) Hardy's dignified remark in his 1902 Preface that he could see nothing exceptionable in his handling of the tragic theme in 'a novel addressed by a man to men and women of full age' suggests his sense that the novel should belong not to the Victorian family fireside but to the mature and responsible reader. In 'Locksley Hall Sixty Years After' in 1885 Tennyson had already denounced the new literary frankness through his aged spokesman:

> Authors – essayist, atheist, novelist, realist, rhymester, play your part,
> Paint the mortal shame of nature with the living hues of Art.

> Rip your brothers' vices open, strip your own foul passions bare;
> Down with Reticence, down with Reverence – forward, naked – let them stare.

> Feed the budding rose of boyhood with the drainage of your sewer;
> Send the drain into the fountain, lest the stream should issue pure.

> Set the maiden fancies wallowing in the troughs of Zolaism, –
> Forward, forward, ay and backward, downward too into the abysm.

Divergent and often conflicting ideas about art and culture are characteristic of the end of the nineteenth century, and this suggests the breakdown of prevailing assumptions, artistic, ethical and social.

The novelist who most consistently strove to create a new form of fiction in English at this time was Henry James (1843–1916). (Hardy, disgusted and upset at the reception of *Jude*, turned after it exclusively to poetry.) Apart from his numerous novels and stories, James also wrote literary criticism in which he showed an intense interest in the technical problems of the novelist's art. This theoretical concern running alongside the practice of the art was itself to be characteristic of Modernism. James noted this change in 'The Art of Fiction' in 1884:

> Only a short time ago it might have been supposed that the English novel was not what the French call *discutable*. It had no air of having a theory, a conviction, a consciousness of itself behind it – of being the expression of an artistic faith, the result of choice and comparison.

James welcomed the change since the era of Dickens and Thackeray when 'there was a comfortable, good-humoured feeling abroad that a novel is a novel, as a pudding is a pudding, and that our only business with it could be to swallow it.' He argued, indeed, that theoretical understanding, such as he found in the French novelists from Flaubert to Zola, was necessary to complete artistic success, and himself provided, in his many reviews and in the Prefaces he wrote for the New York edition of his novels (1906–7), the most sustained criticism of the novel in English. It is not surprising to find him challenging many Victorian assumptions about the novel.

In 'The Art of Fiction' James criticized the tendency for Victorian novelists to break into their novels by some form of direct statement:

> I was lately struck, in reading over many pages of Anthony Trollope, with his want of discretion in this particular. In a digression, a parenthesis or an aside, he concedes to the reader that he and this trusting friend are only 'making believe'. He admits that the events he narrates have not really happened, and

that he can give his narrative any turn the reader may like best. Such a betrayal of a sacred office seems to me, I confess, a terrible crime . . .

James is here insisting, in what may now seem a naïve way, that the novelist must take seriously his role as a truth-teller. The easy-going relationship with the public is replaced by an austere responsibility to the work itself. And in relation to that work, James' emphasis is on unity:

A novel is a living thing, all one and continuous, like any other organism, and in proportion as it lives will it be found, that in each of the parts there is something of each of the other parts.

Here James is applying the language of the Romantic critics, especially Coleridge, to the novel. The concern with organic unity remained central for him, and led him away later from Victorian conventions. But he always argued that unity did not mean simply selecting a limited range of material; on the contrary, fiction was animated by the attempt to catch 'the note and trick, the strange irregular rhythm of life.' Finally, he wittily took issue with complacency about the moral purity of the English novel, asserting 'not that the English novel has a purpose, but that it has a diffidence.' It avoids, that is to say, dangerous topics, particularly those concerned with sexual behaviour, in order to retain its purity, which turns out to be morally vacuous. Thus in respect to authorial intrusion and to the evasiveness resulting from the ethical consensus, James is critical of the conventional novel, and advocates a deeper kind of unity as his ideal.

In his critical prefaces, published as *The Art of the Novel* by R. P. Blackmur, James discusses his own work and his attempts to solve the problems arising from the limitations of the Victorian novel. Probably the best-known single passage is in the preface to *The Tragic Muse*:

A picture without composition slights its most precious chance for beauty, and is moreover not composed at all unless the painter knows *how* that principle of health and safety, working as an

absolutely premeditated art, has prevailed. There may in its
absence be life, incontestably, as *The Newcomes* has life, as *Les
Trois Mousquetaires*, as Tolstoy's *War and Peace*, have it; but what
do such large loose baggy monsters, with their queer elements of
the accidental and the arbitrary, artistically *mean*? ... There is life
and life, and as waste is only life sacrificed and thereby prevented
from 'counting', I delight in a deep-breathing economy and an
organic form.

The analogy with pictorial composition is used to insist upon the
necessity for aesthetic unity in a novel. In fact Victorian painters had
been as profuse of detail as Victorian novelists, but just as Whistler
was creating a strikingly harmonious pictorial art, so James aimed at
the unified novel. Thackeray, Dumas, Tolstoy: the grouping now
seems curious, but is presumably to suggest the widespread tendency for nineteenth-century novels to be what James called
*Middlemarch*, 'a treasure-house of detail but ... an indifferent
whole.'

The idea of unity, of organic form, is central to James' thinking
about the novel. But he does not seek this unity in what might
seem the simplest way: by writing only short novels, or stories on
single subjects (though he sometimes does this). What he values
about the novel is certainly not its exclusiveness; he often emphasizes
its variety as a merit, as in the preface to *The Portrait of a Lady*:

Here we get exactly the high price of the novel as a literary form
– its power ... to appear most true to its character in proportion
as it strains, or tends to burst, with a latent extravagance, its
mould.

James goes further here than his predecessors in stressing the variety
of personal responses which may occur, the subjectivity of each
individual observer of the human scene:

He and his neighbours are watching the same show, but one
seeing more where the other sees less, one seeing black where
the other sees white, one seeing big where the other sees small,
one seeing coarse where the other sees fine.

Victorian writers would have been disturbed by the subjectivism of this; James rejoices in it ('there is fortunately no saying on what, for the particular pair of eyes, the window may *not* open'). But the admission that the world is different for different observers poses urgent problems for the artist who is preoccupied with unity. How is he to unify the divergent elements which he knows to constitute life itself, especially when he is aware that each consciousness experiences life differently? James' answer is what Blackmur calls the Fine Central Intelligence. In *The Portrait of a Lady* that Intelligence (I would prefer to call it a Consciousness) is Isabel Archer. James describes how he saw her as the answer to his problem of focus:

> 'Place the centre of the subject in the young woman's own consciousness,' I said to myself, 'and you get as interesting and as beautiful a difficulty as you could wish. Stick to *that* – for the centre; put the heaviest weight into *that* scale, which will be so largely the scale of her relation to herself.'

Through the use of such a character James solved the problem of unity without surrendering the possibility of complexity. He goes beyond the simple concept of a unity achieved by having one central character, as in, say, *Tom Jones*, by making the consciousness of that character fine enough to constitute the central interest of the novel. This was to be his method in such large-scale novels as *The Portrait of a Lady* and *The Ambassadors*. But in *The Golden Bowl* (1907) James went further, giving the first part of the novel to the Prince and the second to the Princess. This is a formal recognition of the fact of subjectivism, but it raises the problem of unity more acutely. In this novel James' solution is to use a central image, the bowl itself, and to have a plot development in which the Princess takes over as the central character. But questions may still arise: why don't we have Mr Verver's consciousness? or Charlotte Stant's? Is the Princess' development due rather to the inner necessity of the novelist's conception than to her own nature? In fact James is very successful in combining unity with a sense of the depth and variety of human consciousness in *The Golden Bowl*, but the problem was to become central for the next generation of novelists. How can a novel simultaneously reflect and express the complexity of life, and achieve the coherence of unity?

Nor was this problem in fact confined to the novel. An attempt to answer it can be seen also in the poetry and criticism of W. B. Yeats, another transitional figure, who began to publish while Tennyson was still Laureate and who was writing poetry up to his death in 1939. In the 1880s the young Yeats found in Aesthetic and Symbolist ideas a welcome antidote to Victorian rhetoric. He rejected outright the 'public' stance in the twilight world of his early poems ('Dream, dream, for this is also sooth'), and in essays like 'The Symbolism of Poetry' (1900) looked forward to a change of poetic method:

> A return to the way of our fathers, a casting out of descriptions of nature for the sake of nature, of the moral law for the sake of the moral law, a casting out of all anecdotes and of that brooding over scientific opinion that so often extinguishes the central flame in Tennyson, and of that vehemence that would make us do or not do certain things.

The change would involve the replacement of the energetic rhythms of the will by 'wavering, meditative, organic rhythms', and a recognition of the supremacy of form. But the Aesthetic or Symbolist position did not satisfy Yeats for long. He began to sense that the rejection of Victorian rhetoric and externalities was leading to a poetry whose purity was anaemic. When his early critical essays were published in 1903 as *Ideas of Good and Evil*, he sent a copy to John Quinn with an interesting letter showing how his attitude was changing:

> I feel that much of it is out of my present mood; that it is true, but no longer true for me ... The book is too lyrical, too full of aspirations after remote things, too full of desires. I have always felt that the soul has two movements primarily: one to transcend

forms, and the other to create forms. Nietzsche, to whom you have been the first to introduce me, calls these the Dionysiac and the Apollonic, respectively. I think I have to some extent got weary of that wild God Dionysus, and I am hoping that the Fire-Darter will come in his place.

Yeats never changed his view that Victorian poetry had lost itself in irrelevancies, but he came to feel that the solution of Symbolism, the creation of a 'pure' poetry, was equally inadequate. In other words, Symbolist poetry achieved the necessary aesthetic unity too easily.

In 'In the Seven Woods' (1903), 'The Green Helmet' (1910) and 'Responsibilities' (1914), Yeats began to create a new kind of poetry in accordance with his changed views. He also wrote very perceptively about the whole situation, especially in the series of short essays called 'Discoveries' (1906). In the section called 'Personality and the Intellectual Essences' he saw the history of literature as a movement away from the energy of a Villon to the more sophisticated but insubstantial appeal of a Shelley.

Although Yeats presents the choice as open, his own sympathy is clearly with the literature represented by Villon. He believes that poetry should be an integrated art, the expression of the whole personality, 'blood, imagination, intellect, running together'. The Symbolists followed the Romantics in their devotion to the imagination; the Victorians, it might be argued, cultivated some forms of intellect; but that elemental force, the blood, had appealed to neither. From this point onward in his career Yeats is always striving to create a poetry with this power of integration, though always aware of the forces in the modern world making for incoherence and confusion. In 'Art and Ideas' (1914) he rejects his early aesthetic belief in a 'pure' art dissociated from ideas, in favour of a 'more profound Pre-Raphaelitism' in which all elements of the artist's personality find expression, a 're-integration of the mind'.

At this point in his career Yeats felt that poetic success was possible only on a small scale. He refers to *The Revolt of Islam*,

*The Excursion, Gebir, The Idylls of the King* and *The Ring and the Book* as lacking the unity of the great poems of the past, and suggested that the unity of Arnold's *Sohrab and Rustrum* is 'a classical imitation and not an organic thing'. True unity on a large scale is impossible:

> Meanwhile it remains for some greater time, living once more in passionate reverie, to create a *King Lear*, a *Divine Comedy*, vast worlds moulded by their own weight like drops of water.

But Yeats was not content to accept this situation for long. In the volumes which he published during the era of Modernism, and especially in *The Tower* (1928), he attempted to solve the problem of the tension between the awareness of complexity and the commitment to unity. In that great sequence of poems from 'Sailing to Byzantium' through 'The Tower', 'Meditations in Time of Civil War', 'Nineteen Hundred and Nineteen', 'Leda and the Swan', 'Among School Children', 'A Man Young and Old', to 'All Soul's Night', the reader is carried through a wide range of experience, both intimately personal and political, from 'That is no country for old men' to the self-confident poetic mind 'Wound in mind's wandering As mummies in the mummy cloth are wound.' The movement is, put crudely, from 'wisdom', through various aspects of life, including a passionate acceptance of its totality in 'Among School Children', back finally to a reassuring 'wisdom' beyond life. But one's strongest sense is of the energy of the individual poems rather than of an overall pattern. Whether a convincing unity is achieved without strain is open to critical discussion: the Modernism of the later Yeats shows itself partly in his concern for such a balance between pattern and experience.

# 2

## The era of Modernism: 1910–1930

Socially the period was one of widespread turmoil and suffering, including the 1914–18 war and the beginning of the economic depression. Yet culturally it was a great creative period, which produced such works as Eliot's *The Waste Land*, Pound's *Hugh Selwyn Mauberley*, Joyce's *Ulysses*, Lawrence's *Women in Love*, Virginia Woolf's *To the Lighthouse*, and Yeats' *The Tower*, to say nothing of the contemporary work of Rilke, Blok, Mayakovsky, Pasternak, Machado, Apollinaire, Ungaretti, Alberti, Mann, Proust, Kafka, and Svevo. And this is in literature alone. The challenge to the artist is always to combine openness to experience with formal control, and the art of this troubled period often thrived on the challenge. The discussion in this section is at first general and then specific, focusing in the later parts on the critical ideas of two leading modernists, Eliot and Virginia Woolf, and ending with two major modernist works, Pound's *Mauberley* and Joyce's *Ulysses*, and with a general account of D. H. Lawrence.

### General considerations

Any ascription of dates to cultural movements is bound to be arbitrary, but there can be little doubt that the two decades 1910–30 constitute an intelligible unity from the point of view of the present discussion. (Obviously historians of politics, war or economics will see the century in a different shape – but that kind of plural vision is one of the central recognitions of Modernism itself.) There can be valid disagreement about the extent of the

interaction between culture and society, but it is evident that
modernist art is very much aware of the state of the world around it.
Thus many kinds of facts about the early twentieth century are
relevant. In general what was happening can be seen as a breaking-
up (more or less violent in different countries and areas of activity)
of the nineteenth-century consensus. Some aspects of this have
already been seen in relation to Henry James and Yeats, but it can be
illustrated from almost every sphere of life. Politically there is the
increasing challenge to Capital by Labour, no longer prepared to
accept a completely subordinate role as the economic benefits of
industrialism became more obvious. Socially this was paralleled in
the efforts of other dominated groups to improve their status: the
feminists are a striking example. The weakening of the idea of sub-
ordination in the more open, flexible and competitive situation of
increased social mobility meant that the old simple verities no longer
seemed true. Accepting one's place, loyalty to authority, un-
questioning obedience, began to break down; patriotism, doing
one's duty, even Christianity, seemed questionable ideals. Man's
understanding of himself was changing. Anthropology was probing
the primitive roots of religion: James Frazer's *The Golden Bough*
appeared in twelve volumes between 1890 and 1915. Philosophers
like Nietzsche and Bergson had already emphasized the importance
of instinct rather than reason. Psychologists like Freud and Jung
were showing the power and significance of the unconscious.
Scientific explanations were becoming more subtle and harder for
the layman to understand. Put in the most simplified and general
terms, it can be said that the world of 1910 was felt to be much
more complex than the world as it had been known before, and
especially more complex than the orderly world that had been
presented to the reader in Victorian literature. The war of 1914–
1918 dramatically crystallized and hastened the changes. The sense
of complexity was to be the modernist writer's fundamental
recognition.

All great writers of whatever period have been aware of complexity, and have incorporated into their works a wide-ranging

understanding of life. But it is arguable that even the most sceptical of them had some unquestioned assumptions which he accepted from the climate of his age; even Swift had the Ancients, even Sterne had Sensibility – and both had God. Some twentieth-century writers have also retained these kinds of unquestioned belief, but to the extent that they have done so their sensibility has not been modernist. (This applies to a great deal of middle-brow writing, but also to a Catholic novelist like Waugh, or a humanist novelist like Orwell.) For the modern western world is less sure of its values than most previous cultures with which we are familiar; relativism and subjectivity are facts of everyday experience. The greater depth of modern scepticism, or awareness of complexity, is shown too in the artist's relation to his art. However strongly Pope may have felt the rush of his society towards anarchy, the chaos of values and the imminence of disaster – all of which he conveys so powerfully in *The Dunciad* – he had no doubts about the heroic couplet. However dark may have been Dickens' intuitions about the future of commercialized England, he did not doubt that the serially published novel could express his vision. In the twentieth century the position was different. Not only did the modernist artist see himself confronted by the infinite complexity of reality, he also saw that his medium itself might be part of the problem.

But it was characteristic of the modernists not to be cowed by this challenge. Stephen Spender in *The Struggle of the Modern* in 1953, one of the most incisive discussions of these issues, made two observations which, taken together, emphasize and clarify the point. First, 'Modern art is that in which the artist reflects awareness of an unprecedented modern situation in form and idiom', and second that 'the principle of reality in our time is peculiarly difficult to grasp, and that "realism" is not an adequate approach to it.' The same point emerges in Eric Auerbach's wide-ranging study of the representation of reality in western literature, *Mimesis* (1946). Auerbach considers a great variety of methods from Homer onwards, and his last chapter, entitled 'The Brown Stocking', focuses on Mrs Ramsay in Virginia Woolf's *To the Lighthouse*. Of this kind of novel, he notes that the author 'submits, much more than was done in earlier realistic works, to the random contingency of real phenomena; and even though he winnows and stylizes the material of the real world – as of course he cannot help doing – he does not proceed rationalistically, nor with a view to bringing a continuity of exterior events to a planned conclusion'. Similarly, in *Ulysses*, Auerbach notes the 'dizzying whirl of motifs, wealth of words and concepts, perpetual playing on their countless associations, and the ever re-aroused but never satisfied doubt as to what order is ultimately hidden behind so much apparent arbitrariness'. The sense of the almost overwhelming abundance of the experience to be made into art marks off Modernism from the rarefied atmosphere of Symbolism and Aestheticism. Nothing could be further removed from the modernist artist's sense of his problems than Oscar Wilde's observation in 'The Critic as Artist' in 1891 that 'The subject-matter at the disposal of creation becomes every day more limited in extent and variety. Providence and Mr Walter Besant have exhausted the obvious.' It was precisely 'the obvious' that was to provide the inexhaustible source of the modernist novel.

If experience was felt to have enormous complexity, it followed, as Spender argued, that traditional realistic methods were inadequate to render it. Thus we have the various experiments in method that characterized the development of Modernism in all the arts. Since these all aimed to get beyond the over-simplified accounts of experience which traditional art was held to give, they necessarily involved new methods of organization, particularly through juxtaposition (rather than simple narrative) and irony (rather than unity of mood). Joseph Frank's important article 'Spatial Form in Modern Literature' in 1945 discussed the decline of chronological narrative structures in modern literature, and its replacement by what he called 'spatial form', the presentation of the unity of a work in 'the entire pattern of internal references', or 'the principle of reflexive reference'. This method Frank found common to *The Waste Land*, *The Cantos*, *Ulysses*, Proust, and Djuna Barnes's *Nightwood*. The reader is being asked not to follow a story but to discern a pattern. Frank noted the inescapable difficulty in this kind of literature, the tension between 'the time-logic of language and the space-logic implicit in the modern conception of the nature of poetry' – and, as he also shows, of the novel.

For some readers and critics this has been the central weakness of Modernism. In its pursuit of a more complex sense of reality, it is felt to have failed in coherence. This is an issue that has been constantly – and, indeed, relevantly – raised throughout the history of Modernism. In 1923 Richard Aldington, one of the early Imagists but a writer whose attitudes became increasingly traditional, raised the issue in his review of *Ulysses*, where he referred to Joyce's 'great undisciplined talent', and in 'The Poet and His Age', where he argued 'that the age is incoherent . . . is no reason why art generally . . . should be incoherent.' Eliot immediately replied in *The Dial* with '*Ulysses*, Order and Myth', suggesting that Joyce was the pioneer of a valuable new method:

> Instead of narrative method, we may now use the mythical method. It is, I seriously believe, a step towards making the modern world possible for art.

This suggests the possibility of achieving coherence in a different way from the conventional narrative method, and is as relevant to Eliot's poetry as to Joyce's novel.

However, myth is available to a modern poet in quite a different way from that in which a primitive man experiences it – it is not a matter of simple acceptance, but of deliberation and selection, which may lead to artificiality. Yeats, who greatly admired Shelley's poetry, nevertheless felt its limitations:

> Intellectual Beauty has not only the happy dead to do her will, but ministering spirits who correspond to the Devas of the East, and the Elemental Spirits of medieval Europe, and the Sidhe of ancient Ireland, and whose too constant presence, and perhaps Shelley's ignorance of their more traditional forms, gives some of his poetry an air of rootless phantasy.

The 'rootless phantasy' is what myths can become if used without sufficient intelligence or urgency. T. S. Eliot made a similar criticism of Blake's prophetic books. Whether this was justified or not, it can certainly be turned onto Eliot himself. Where was the principle of order to be found? It is significant that Eliot was able to find an answer in the Anglican tradition, and so to write a work of criticism like *After Strange Gods* in 1931, with the subtitle 'A Primer of Modern Heresy'. Few other modern artists have, however, been able to accept a traditional religious solution to the problem of values and order, and even in Eliot's more orthodox later poetry the sceptical modernist intelligence is always there to place Christian theology under a strenuous challenge – just as it is there in Yeats, asserting the temporal values of the self against the Byzantine abstractions of the soul.

The use of myth is one way in which the modernist writer has felt able to give coherence to his work, the myths often being of the most general kind, concerned with death and regeneration, the cycle of nature, the order of the seasons, though sometimes, as in the case of *Ulysses*, more specifically literary. But there are other ways of achieving unity in modernist works. For example, an analogy with music was used by I. A. Richards in 1924 to suggest the ordering principle of *The Waste Land*:

> ... his poetry a 'music of ideas'. The ideas are of all kinds, abstract and concrete, general and particular, and, like the musician's phrases, they are arranged, not that they may tell us something, but that their effects in us may combine into a coherent whole of feeling and attitude and produce a peculiar liberation of the will.

In *A Survey of Modernist Poetry* in 1927, Laura Riding and Robert Graves put a similar argument through a different analogy:

> The whole trend of modern poetry is toward treating poetry like a sensitive substance which succeeds better when allowed to crystallize by itself than when put into prepared moulds ... Modern poetry, that is, is groping for some principle of self-

determination, to be applied to the making of the poem – not lack of government but government from within.

They went on to contrast the essential unity of *The Waste Land* with the adventitious unity of *In Memoriam*, ascribed simply to 'metrical regularity.' A parallel contrast was made by Herbert Read in *Form in Modern Poetry* in 1932, contrasting 'organic' with 'abstract' form:

> [Organic form is] the form imposed on poetry by the laws of its own origination, without consideration of the given forms of traditional poetry. It is the most original and most vital principle of poetic creation; and the distinction of modern poetry is to have recovered the principle.

The defence of Modernism, that is to say, has always included the assertion that its successful works embody a principle of coherence or order which is more subtle, complex, and ultimately satisfying, because more adequate to contemporary reality, than established methods.

Equally logically, its opponents from Aldington onwards have always denied its coherence. Auerbach raised the question whether modernist approaches were 'a symptom of the confusion and help-lessness ... a mirror of the decline of our world.' His own answer was inconclusive, but plenty of voices have been raised to give an affirmative reply. Some of these are discussed in the last part of this book. The issue is so important that it cannot be solved by any simple assertion; the reader is asked to keep its centrality in mind.

One characteristic of Modernism, then, is an acute awareness of the problems of art, an unremitting self-consciousness. Evidence of this may be seen in the energy and variety of the criticism that accompanied and presumably assisted the development of modern-ist literature. Magazines played a very important part in making the new ideas about art current in the intellectual life of the time. They included A. R. Orage's *New Age*, Ford Madox Ford's *English Review*, Richard Aldington's *Egoist*, Ezra Pound and Wyndham Lewis' *Blast* and later Lewis' *Enemy*, Edgell Rickword's *Calendar of*

*Modern Letters*, Middleton Murry's *Athenaeum* and later his *Adelphi*, Eliot's *Criterion* and F. R. Leavis' *Scrutiny*. Unlike their Victorian predecessors, many of them were short-lived. But as their function, too, was different – to introduce new work and new ideas about art rather than to apply accepted standards – they can be seen as influential to different degrees. Important volumes of criticism were also published, often drawing on material from the magazines. This criticism included Eliot's *The Sacred Wood* (1920), Percy Lubbock's *Craft of Fiction* (1921), Murry's *Problem of Style* (1922), T. E. Hulme's *Speculations* edited by Herbert Read (1924), I. A. Richards' *Principles of Literary Criticism* (1924), Eliot's *Homage to John Dryden* (1924), Virginia Woolf's *The Common Reader* (1925), Edwin Muir's *Transition* (1926), Laura Riding and Robert Graves' *Survey of Modernist Poetry* (1927), E. M. Forster's *Aspects of the Novel* (1927), Eliot's *For Lancelot Andrewes* (1928), Richards' *Practical Criticism* (1929), Muir's *Structure of the Novel* (1929), William Empson's *Seven Types of Ambiguity* (1930), Wilson Knight's *Wheel of Fire* (1930) and *The Imperial Theme* (1931), Edmund Wilson's *Axël's Castle* (1931) and Leavis' *New Bearings in English Poetry* (1932). In all this criticism the emphasis falls on the inclusiveness of the sensibility to be expressed in the work, with its concomitant demands on the reader; and on the subtlety of the ordering process which is nevertheless the basis of value. It might be argued that these critical ideas are not new; that they can be paralleled in many of the Romantic critics, especially Coleridge. But Modernism is very much more self-conscious about its own techniques. Shelley's 'profuse strains of unpremeditated art' suggest a reliance on inspiration, shared also by Blake, of which Coleridge offers a quieter version in his idea of subordinating art to nature. Such an antithesis was hardly possible for the modernist artist, acutely aware that human consciousness provides his primary if not his only data.

The characteristic demandingness of Modernism arose from the writers' sense of the difficulty of their task. Only a complex and demanding art, it was felt, could adequately render a modern consciousness of the world. This feeling can be accounted for in several ways. It can be said that all great art is complex, and that pre-modernist criticism – say, A. C. Bradley on Shakespearean tragedy – was misleading in its simplifications. Or that the modern world *is* more complex than previous forms of society, owing to the effects of a technology which has not only filled the world with more 'things' than ever before, but also changed the relatively settled relationships of the feudal era for the confused openness of the modern industrial state. Or it could be argued that the consciousness of the modern artist has been rendered more self-directed by the influence of psychological investigation, revealing the complexity of the human personality, and of philosophical enquiry, emphasizing the role of the agent in creating the reality which he experiences. The decline of respect for authority is another aspect of the situation. Many of these trends had been developing over a long time-scale; it is probably too limiting to trace them back only as far as the Romantic period. Yet they reached a peculiar urgency in the early twentieth century, and modernist art was one result: its complexity is innate, irremovable.

It is in poetry and the novel that Modernism can first be most clearly discerned. At least in English and American literature, on which this account is focused, developments in drama followed a different course. The influence of Bernard Shaw certainly moved drama away from some nineteenth-century conventions, but the methods which he used instead were consistent with a rationalistic philosophy. The more radical innovations of the later Ibsen, and of Strindberg and Pirandello, had no immediate influence in England. Brecht's combination of technical innovation with a strong political and moral emphasis was more readily accepted in the thirties, but led to no major work. His insistence on the 'alienation effect' in order to force the audience into judgment rather than identification paralleled the modernist repudiation of simple responses, but was far more definite and conclusive in intention. The post-1945 work of Arthur Miller and Tennessee Williams in America, and later of John Osborne and Arnold Wesker in England, also tended towards the direct representation of social experience rather than the complexities of Modernism. Only with the plays of Samuel Beckett and Eugene Ionesco, followed creatively by Harold Pinter, did the drama take a form recognizably modernist. But because of the dates of these developments and their parallels in the other arts, it might be argued – in terms discussed in the final section of this book – that drama has a less significant palaeo-modernist phase, and a more significant neo-modernist one. The reasons for this must remain debatable, but the social nature of the theatre as an institution must be among them.

The following specific discussions should both exemplify the variety and complexity of Modernism and suggest the common elements which justify the use of the term.

## Specific discussions

### T. S. Eliot's early criticism

The acceptance of a modernist view of poetry in England was certainly accelerated by the influence of Eliot's early criticism, the restrained and elegant manner of which could persuade readers who rejected Ezra Pound's more polemical assertion of similar attitudes. Eliot's volume of essays *The Sacred Wood* appeared in 1920, two years before the best known and most discussed of modernist poems, *The Waste Land*, so that the bases of the new poetic were asserted early. And the central concern of *The Sacred Wood* was, as Eliot put it in his Preface to the 1928 edition, 'the problem of the integrity of poetry', to show the essential nature of poetry as distinguished from other forms of knowledge or discourse. In doing this, Eliot found it necessary to re-define the nature of criticism. The book opens with a brief polemical introduction followed by a number of short articles and reviews rearranged to form two chapters: 'The Perfect Critic' and 'Imperfect Critics'. Arthur Symons appears as the 'impressionistic critic' for whom the evocation of impressions serves as 'the satisfaction of a suppressed creative wish'. He cannot further the discussion of literature because his assertions are not about plays or poems but about the feelings which they arouse in him, and as such, Eliot argues, they are essentially unverifiable. Such critics offer an inferior substitute for art, for 'Their sensibility alters the object, but never transforms it.' George Wyndham, 'A Romantic Aristocrat' among 'Imperfect Critics' is shown to have turned the discussion of literature into the re-creation, splendidly but fatally unselfconscious, of a private world in which poetry, hunting and the politics of Imperialism are 'one and the same thing':

> Romanticism is a short cut to the strangeness [of life] without the reality, and it leads its disciples only back upon themselves. George Wyndham had curiosity, but he employed it romantically, not to penetrate the real world but to complete the varied features of the world he made for himself.

Swinburne, discussed in the same chapter, is seen as immune to these temptations because his poetry has satisfied his emotional needs; he remains, however, 'an appreciator and not a critic'. Eliot implies that the absence of any critical awareness concerning his own poetic left Swinburne without the necessary motive for pressing an enquiry into the workings of sensibility in poets of another age, specifically the Jacobeans. He lacked the intellectual energy for the enterprise which Eliot himself was to sustain from about 1917 up to the publication of *Homage to John Dryden* – the kind of energy associated with the 'superior sensibility' of 'The Perfect Critic' (who is nearly but not quite identified with Remy de Gourmont):

> ... for sensibility wide and profound reading does not mean merely a more extended pasture. There is not merely an increase of understanding, leaving the original acute impression unchanged. The new impressions modify the impressions received from the objects already known. An impression needs to be constantly refreshed by new impressions in order that it may persist at all; it needs to take its place in a system of impressions.

In the mind of the real critic impressions generalize themselves:

> ... the true generalization is not something superposed upon an accumulation of perceptions; the perceptions do not, in a really appreciative mind, accumulate as a mass, but form themselves as a structure; and criticism is the statement in language of this structure; it is a development of sensibility.

Rather than an account of what happens in the work of Arnold, de Gourmont, or any other critic, Eliot is here offering a description of the ideal condition which he is attempting to realize. The suggestion of a striving for finality and theoretical completeness conveyed by 'the statement in language of this structure' is a defiant signal of his intention to break with the tradition of *belles-lettres*, although it perhaps gives an impression of closing discussion when much remains unexplained. This is a feature of Eliot's criticism which should be emphasized; the reader does not necessarily have to admit the finality which the style of some of the more controversial pronouncements claims for them. For these essays are concerned with central critical issues about which there must be the possibility of disagreement.

However, Eliot's intention, carried out with persistency and wit, is to assert a system of values for poetry which emphasizes impersonality, a denial of the supposedly Romantic assumption that a poet's main function is to express himself. Eliot shows how much more complex a process is involved. The most important essay from his point of view is 'Tradition and the Individual Talent', which Eliot chose to place first in his *Selected Essays* in 1932 and subsequently. This contains an aphoristic rejection of the idea of self-expression:

> Poetry is not a turning loose of emotion, but an escape from emotion; it is not the expression of personality, but an escape from personality.

This argument is backed up by an emphasis on tradition, for the artist who is aware of his place in a tradition must be concerned with something other than his own personal emotions. Indeed for Eliot, 'The progress of an artist is a continual self-sacrifice, a continual extinction of personality.' This emphasis on 'depersonalization' is backed up by the use of a scientific analogy: the action of creating poetry is compared to the action occurring when 'a bit of finely filiated platinum is introduced into a chamber containing oxygen and sulphur dioxide.' The analogy, the reader is told, is that of the catalyst: the platinum must be present if the two gases are to form sulphurous acid, but the platinum remains 'inert, neutral, and unchanged.' Similarly the artist's mind, it is suggested, is simply a catalyst for inducing significant combinations of emotions and feelings. In fact analogies are logically inconclusive, and this one may seem of doubtful relevance. But the point is emphatically made that the interest of readers of poetry should be not in the mind of the artist but in the result of the creative process. Indeed, Eliot goes so far as to assert that 'the more perfect the artist, the more completely separate in him will be the man who suffers and the mind which creates.' Yeats would have denied this, but its assertion clears the way for a poetry which appeals to us not by the simplicity of its assertions but by the complexity of its coherence.

Other essays in *The Sacred Wood* concern Marlowe, Jonson and Massinger, suggesting Eliot's interest in the Elizabethan and Jacobean drama as having embodied qualities which he considered of significance in the early twentieth century. But it is the essay on 'Hamlet and his Problems' which, in passing an adverse judgment on that play so popular with the Romantic critics, included a formulation that has become widely known:

The only way of expressing emotion in the form of art is by finding an 'objective correlative'; in other words, a set of objects, a situation, a chain of events which shall be the formula of that *particular* emotion; such that when the external facts, which must terminate in sensory experience, are given, the emotion is immediately evoked.

The process by which the writer's emotion is expressed is thus an indirect one. He does not merely announce his feelings, he renders them fully and delicately through the appropriate 'set of objects . . . situation . . . chain of events'. This gives an important insight into the way that modernist poems and novels often work, their structure expressing an emotion rather than putting forward an argument. And it also makes clear, what is sometimes not recognized in Eliot's criticism, that the final value is emotion rather than some classical idea of order. That Eliot's sense of tradition is as a living continuity can be felt in all these essays, as in the formulation at the end of his account of Swinburne's poetry:

> His language is not, like the language of bad poetry, dead. It is very much alive, with this singular life of its own. But the language which is more important to us is that which is struggling to digest and express new objects, new groups of objects, new feelings, new aspects, as, for instance, the prose of Mr James Joyce or the early Conrad.

In the best of these essays Eliot gives a strong sense of his own commitment to a poetry that will succeed in the struggle 'to digest and express new objects . . .'.

This continuity of concern is suggested also by the title of Eliot's next critical book, *Homage to John Dryden* (1924). In it Eliot not only defended a poet generally stigmatized during the nineteenth century as prosaic, as part of the attempt to widen the area available for treatment in poetry, but also put forward a lucid and challenging view of the English poetic tradition in the essays 'The Metaphysical Poets' and 'Andrew Marvell'. The former took the poetry of Donne as exemplifying the activity of mind characteristic of the highest achievement:

> A thought to Donne was an experience; it modified his sensibility. When a poet's mind is perfectly equipped for its work, it is constantly amalgamating disparate experience; the ordinary man's experience is chaotic, irregular, fragmentary. The latter falls in love, or reads Spinoza, and these two experiences have

nothing to do with each other, or with the noise of the typewriter or the smell of cooking; in the mind of the poet these experiences are always forming new wholes.

This again shows the modernist desire for inclusiveness, for literary forms that can bring together the full complexity of experience in a meaningful way. Eliot went on to suggest an historical theory, that of 'the dissociation of sensibility'. According to this, in the seventeenth century occurred a change from the comprehensiveness which Eliot exemplifies in quotations from Chapman and King and Lord Herbert, to the kind of effect Eliot finds in Tennyson, in which thought and emotion have become separated. This development, encouraged in different ways by Milton and Dryden, Eliot believes to have enfeebled subsequent poetry. The essay 'Andrew Marvell' is based on the same assumption. Marvell is praised for his wit or urbanity, which is said to give his poetry a maturity not to be found in the Romantics and their Victorian followers, preoccupied with 'the effort to construct a dream world'. This again indicates Eliot's belief that poetry should deal, although on its own terms, with the life of its time in all its fullness. Scholars and critics, like Frank Kermode in *Romantic Image* (1957), have argued that the idea of a dissociation of sensibility is historically invalid; it seems unlikely that there would be one single point in a culture at which so radical a change could occur. But at all events, the force of Eliot's argument is rather in the idea that its historical focus, and the idea of poetry as expressing an undissociated, or unified, sensibility is what is significant. It can be seen as parallel to Yeats's insistence on 'blood, imagination, intellect, running together'. Modernist art in general tries to restore this fullness of expression.

Eliot continued to write critical prose, particularly in *The Criterion*, which he edited from 1922 to 1939. But it gradually came to be more concerned with social and general cultural issues, as he noted as early as the Preface to *For Lancelot Andrewes* (1928). (He had entered the Church of England in 1927.) The sub-title of that volume, 'Essays on Style and Order', suggest a changing emphasis.

And in the account of Lancelot Andrewes, Bishop of Winchester, who died in 1626, an interesting contrast is drawn with Donne, with reference to the sermons of the two preachers:

> Donne is a 'personality' in a sense in which Andrewes is not: his sermons, one feels, are a 'means of self-expression'. He is constantly finding an object which shall be adequate to his feelings; Andrewes is wholly absorbed in the object and therefore responds with the adequate emotion.

Eliot is careful to say that he is not passing judgment here, merely describing the difference between a medieval and a modern sensibility. But the terms of the description are weighted in favour of Andrewes in a way that suggests the development of Eliot's outlook. The criterion of self-expression remains a negative one; but the attitude that is now being 'placed' in Donne ('constantly finding an object ... adequate to his feelings') is similar to that of the artist in the 'Hamlet' essay. Now, it is suggested, there may be a subject-matter whose primary importance will assert itself to the responsive mind in a way that will preclude conscious search. In other words, an orthodox religious sensibility is now seen as a high type of humanity, while Donne 'is not wholly without kinship to Huysmans' – the French Decadent novelist.

The subjects of the essays in the volume suggest the change of emphasis towards political and social matters; they include Machiavelli, F. H. Bradley and 'The Humanism of Irving Babbitt'. Perhaps the account of Baudelaire shows this new development most clearly. Eliot sees the significance of Baudelaire as rooted in his spiritual perceptiveness:

> In the middle nineteenth century, the age which (at its best) Goethe had prefigured, an age of bustle, programmes, platforms, scientific progress, humanitarianism and revolutions which improved nothing, an age of progressive degradation, Baudelaire perceived that what really matters is Sin and Redemption.

This leads on to the paradoxical – and, to the humanist, meaningless claim that Baudelaire was 'man enough for damnation', setting the poet's achievement in the context of his spiritual condition. Here we see the Anglican Eliot who sub-titled his next critical book, *After Strange Gods* (1933), 'A Primer of Modern Heresy' and argued in 'Religion and Literature' (1935) that 'Literary criticism should be completed by criticism from a definite ethical and theological standpoint.' However different his conservative social philosophy may have been from that of the left-wing writers of the thirties, Eliot's work in that decade places a similar emphasis on social and ideological questions. Eliot's commitment to the Anglican tradition had a deliberation about it which precluded him from any facile line of thought. Nevertheless, it can be argued that, both as a critic and a poet, Eliot moved away from his early Modernism as he sought to give expression to a sensibility whose orthodoxy became as important to him as its complexity. But in his early criticism he had given currency to ideas that remain central to the understanding of Modernism.

## Virginia Woolf's critical essays, by Anthony Fothergill

Virginia Woolf's essays, comprising over 350 reviews, critical articles and papers, the most important now collected in four volumes, cover a broad range of literary and non-literary topics – from not knowing Greek to the attractions of Wembley and the niceties of angling. This present discussion will be limited to essays, mainly in the first two volumes, concerned with the traditional and modern novel and their problematic interrelation. It will thus involve three closely-linked areas: the criticism levelled by Virginia Woolf against the subject-matter and forms of the novels by her immediate predecessors who follow in the tradition of eighteenth- and nineteenth-century novelists; the possibilities she envisaged for the development of the novel genre and those qualities in contemporary writers she characterizes as modernist; and finally the nature of the traditional relationship between novelist and reader and text, which undergoes such a radical modification in the twentieth century as a result of the modernist experiment in the novel.

This enterprise is clearly a hazardous one – and for at least three reasons. The first is the historicity of Virginia Woolf's reading of past literature. The essays can only indicate to us how one of the major figures in twentieth-century literature interpreted her literary tradition and how she saw the role of her contemporaries in terms of it. Reading and criticism were for her peculiarly creative activities; she regarded her critical essays as attempts at re-creating past works, re-vitalizing and redeeming the past, and not as 'objective analyses'. Accepting Virginia Woolf's awareness of the historicity of interpretation we too should see the essays and the kinds of questions they ask of earlier novelists, the possibilities they foresee for the modern novel, as attempts at self-understanding on the part of a writer in the early decades of the century faced with the dilemma, as she saw it, of an absence of models to guide the experimental fervour of writers searching for alternative forms to express their changed relation to the world, their acute sense of a shift of sensibility. The essays, in other words, do not offer an 'unmediated' view of the 'object' of her criticism – indeed these very terms become problematic, presupposing a neutrality and objectivity of consciousness (among other things), the question-ability of which is a common modernist theme.

A second hazard lies in the possible but misleading assumption that Virginia Woolf's critical views can be identified with her inten-tions and actual achievements in her novels, in terms of which they are often read. The essays may show us what she *thought* about modern fiction; they will not necessarily reveal the principles by which her own fiction can best be defined. The famous lines from her essay 'Modern Fiction' (1919), for example, are an almost obligatory quotation in any discussion on the nature of the modern novel. They are usually taken by critics, whether they are attacking or defending her, as defining the 'impressionist' method of 'stream of consciousness' novels, the novels of introspective egoism, which Virginia Woolf's own novels are thought to exemplify:

Look within and life, it seems, is very far from being 'like this'. Examine for a moment an ordinary mind on an ordinary day. The mind receives a myriad impressions – trivial, fantastic, evanescent, or engraved with the sharpness of steel. From all sides they come, an incessant shower of innumerable atoms; and as they fall, as they shape themselves into the life of Monday or Tuesday, the accent falls differently from of old; the moment of importance came not here but there ... Life is not a series of gig lamps symmetrically arranged; life is a luminous halo, a semi-transparent envelope surrounding us from the beginning of consciousness to the end.

And after the 'myriad impressionism' the references usually end with the call to arms:

Let us record the atoms as they fall upon the mind in the order in which they fall, let us trace the pattern, however disconnected and incoherent in appearance, which each sight or incident scores upon the consciousness.

Understood as emphasizing a shift in concentration from the representation of the external world to a reflection of the texture of consciousness, understood as asserting the mind's activity in perceiving the world as constituting a, perhaps *the*, most important area of novelistic enquiry, characterizing a general tendency in modern literature to focus on the contents of a character's mind, the inner, mental life of the experiencing subject, the passage is making an important point. But understood, as it so often is, as a manifesto descriptive of literary modernism, read as a rallying-cry for 'stream of consciousness' writers, the passage stands in sharp contradistinction not only to other essays by Virginia Woolf but also the whole tenor of a novel like *The Waves*. For the passage suggests that 'novels are the outbursts of spontaneous inspiration' (a view she strongly disputes in her essay 'On Re-reading Novels') and that the writer's task is recording the passive reception of impressions by the mind without tampering with or manipulating these impressions. Yet again and again in her essays she stresses the importance of recognizing that novels, like other works of art, are artefacts, made through the selection and imposition of structure on material, subject to the choices the novelist makes, the techniques of presentation he adopts:

> We have not named and therefore presumably not recognized the simplest of devices by which every novel has come into being. We have not taken the pains to watch our story-teller as he decides which method he will use . . .

In those essays which discuss a provisional theory of reception, a clear rebuttal can be found of the view that novels, even her own, can be described as 'impressionistic' rejections of the 'well-made novel'.

But as the issue of 'recording the atoms as they fall' is handled by Virginia Woolf in her novels the problem is not just one of method, but an epistemological dilemma. Consciousness, as James and Joyce had shown before her, is not the passive reception of impulses from the outer world but is creative; perception itself, and not just its representation in novels, is intentional, implying the activity of making meaning, structuring reality. As Bernard in *The Waves* realizes, it is not simply a problem of the artistic temperament's will to form which belies or distorts the 'phantom', the flux of reality; it is the very act of perception, of consciousness, of understanding world, which involves structuring:

> I took my mind, my being, the old dejected, almost inanimate object, and lashed it about among these odds and ends, sticks and straws . . . It is the effort and the struggle, it is the perpetual warfare, it is the shattering and piecing together – this is the daily battle . . . The trees, scattered, put on order; the thick green of the leaves thinned itself into a dancing light.

Bernard recognizes the need to create coherence – and the restriction this imposes:

> But in order to make you understand, to give you my life, I must tell a story – and there are so many, and so many . . .

As Gombrich in *Art and Illusion* puts it: 'There is no reality without interpretation' and it is only through the recognition of this that a sense of the gap between world and world as it is perceived may be achieved – a sense of double vision Virginia Woolf discerns in the work of Proust, and which is a major preoccupation of modernist explorers of consciousness such as Joyce and Rilke.

A third hazard is any suggestion of systematic theory. There seems an inherent contradiction between seeing Virginia Woolf's essays as the slow development of a 'theoretical position' on modern writers, and the individuality and spontaneity that being a modern writer entails. Modern*ism*, that is, embodies a logical contradiction. Yet as we may be beginning to realize, paradox and doubt of this sort, difficulty and hazard, have a central place in the linguistic terminology of modernism. The suspicion of system, the desire to resist prescribing norms, is another motif which the reader of Virginia Woolf's works will hear constantly echoing.

'I mistrust all systematizers and I avoid them. The will to a system is a lack of integrity.' Thus Nietzsche. Virginia Woolf shares his hostility towards closed systems – her preference is for the 'openness' of a Henry James text, its indeterminacy – and this hostility finds a characteristically sharp expression in her comments on D. H. Lawrence:

> ... in the Letters he can't listen beyond a point; must give advice; get you into the system too. Hence his attraction for those who want to be fitted: which I don't ... His ruler coming down and measuring [people]. Why all this criticism of other people? Why not some system that includes the good? What a discovery that would be – a system that did not shut out.
>
> ('A Writer's Diary', 2 Oct. 1932)

This attack on system-builders may stand as a warning to us against imposing (or indeed seeing Woolf as imposing) a structure of categories on modernist writers which would belie their own sense of particularity. More specifically it may indicate the danger of believing we have found a coherent prescriptive 'theory of the modern novel' in her critical writings. While she generalizes about tendencies in the 'traditional' and 'modern' novel, she is clearly aware of the tension between general and particular, theory and practice. Indeed one of the abiding impressions of the critical essays is of the emphasis placed on asserting the openness of the novel genre, the possibility to explore through it areas hitherto uncontemplated:

> ... in ten or fifteen years' time prose will be used for purposes for which prose has never been used before. We shall be forced to invent new names for the different books which masquerade under this one heading [of novel].

> ('The Narrow Bridge of Art', 1927)

Nevertheless, if Virginia Woolf is reluctant to dictate the forms the novel genre might adopt, the direction of her argument on the predicament confronting her literary contemporaries is one which tends to blur the differences which exist between them and stress their similarities of position if not of response. This unresolvable tension between generality and particularity is apparent in the essay often cited as her most vigorous exposition of the modern writer's predicament in his rejection of the literary norms and conventions of his immediate 'materialist' predecessors – 'Mr Bennett and Mrs Brown', which was first delivered in May 1924 as a paper read to the Heretics, in Cambridge, under the title 'Character in Fiction'.

She describes her contemporaries as representing a 'camp' of 'Georgian' writers – she refers specifically to Forster, Lawrence, Strachey, Joyce and Eliot – who reject the aesthetic norms and ideological preoccupations of their 'materialist' predecessors such as Wells, Bennett and Galsworthy. This latter group has

> developed a technique of novel-writing which suits their purpose; they have made tools and established conventions which do their business. But those tools are not our tools, and that business is not our business. For us those conventions are ruin, those tools are death.

The conventions signify death because they fail to provide the proper language in terms of which the Georgians' changed sense of reality, their shift in sensibility, might be expressed. What the Edwardian 'materialists' failed to recognize was that 'in or about December 1910, human character changed'. That the first exhibition of Post-Impressionists in Britain took place at the Grafton Galleries in December 1910, is not, perhaps, without interest. But it is not so much to the artistic influence of a Cézanne that Virginia Woolf attributes this change as to more general tendencies:

> All human relations have shifted – those between masters and servants, husbands and wives, parents and children. And when human relations change there is at the same time a change in religion, conduct, politics and literature.

In an early draft of this essay, in the unpublished Monks House papers, Virginia Woolf is far more explicit in attributing this shift in relations to the ideas of Freud, the reading of whose revolutionary accounts of human psychology was absorbing the intelligentsia of the day:

> If you read Freud you know in ten minutes some facts ... or at least some possibilities ... which our parents could not possibly have guessed for themselves [about the ambitions and motives of their fellow creatures].

In her marginal corrections she casts doubts on such a direct attribution – 'that is a very debatable point' she says; 'how much can we make our own from science [?]' – but she remains emphatic on the main point that the modern apprehension of the world and human relations in it is different from the old; that one of the forms this has taken is a far greater interest in the psychological landscape of men; and that the change must needs be registered on the level of literary expression, which requires a new language of forms to embody it.

So Virginia Woolf sees the opening-up of the novel genre, the freeing of the novelist from the traditional constraints of plot, chronological linearity, portrayal of character in the accepted sense, and the exploration of new forms of novel, as an encouragement to a more creative, critical consciousness in novelist and reader. In this new novel, the kind of scepticism a critical reader will bring to the novels of the realists ('Is this all? and if this is all, is it enough? Must we then believe this?' as she puts it in 'Phases of Fiction' in 1929) is consciously activated, and creative resistances are established which make the act of reading also an act of self-understanding. Difficulty and indeterminacy or opacity of meaning are qualities these new novels may possess. Reflexion is what they will provoke.

It is in the novels of Henry James and Proust particularly that Virginia Woolf finds the conscious reappraisal of the principles by which the traditional novel has worked and the exercise of the freedom in choice of subject-matter and therefore in technique which adherence to the traditional novel form had denied the Edwardians. For her their decisive features are two-fold. First, they signal a fundamental shift of perspective from an interest in the world of objects, the world as object, to an examination primarily of the mind perceiving them, of reactions evoked by the objects (which may be things, events or other people), to reveal 'the infinite range and complexity of human sensibility'.

> The visual sense which has thitherto been so active, perpetually sketching fields and farmhouses and faces, seems now to fail or to use its powers to illumine the mind within rather than the world without. Henry James has to find an equivalent for the processes of the mind, to make concrete a mental state.

> ('Phases of Fiction')

Secondly, the techniques practised by James and Proust demand of the reader a far more active participation in understanding the work, so that

> the mind is freed from the perpetual demand of the novelist that we shall feel with his characters. By cutting off the responses which are called out in the actual life, the novelist frees us to

take delight ... in things in themselves. We can see the strangeness of them only when habit has ceased to immerse us in them ... Then we see the mind at work; we are amused by its power to make patterns...

and so as readers
we are at once conscious of using faculties hitherto dormant, ingenuity and skill, a mental nimbleness and dexterity such as serve to solve a puzzle ingeniously.

Both James and Proust are investigating areas of the mind which have hitherto gone unexamined in the novel and so anticipate the direction towards 'the dark places of psychology' Woolf sees the modernist novel taking – not to investigate characters in terms of the morality of their actions and motivations, but to examine the nature of human sensibility and perception. That this change in emphasis has implications for the form of the novel is clear:
The usual supports, the props and struts of the conventions, expressed or observed by the writer, are removed. Everything seems aloof from interference, thrown open to discussion and light, though resting on no visible support.

The openness, the indeterminacy of the novel, its drawing attention to itself as a work of art, the difficulty the reader has in assimilating it, and thus the questioning and doubt and exhilaration it calls forth, are all qualities Woolf finds in Proust and James. As readers,

We cannot rest satisfied but want to experiment further with these extraordinary perceptions, to understand more and more...

It would clearly have been self-contradictory for Virginia Woolf to have stipulated what form the new novel should take. Much of the irrelevant criticisms written on modernist novelists like Joyce and Woolf is based on the mistake of working with a series of concepts and definitions won from the reading of eighteenth- and nineteenth-century novels and applied to novels which are consciously, almost 'thematically', seeking to stretch or explode the limits of the novel genre. Virginia Woolf's own speculations on a new name for the kind of 'novel' she is writing, which she envisages, and the weary amusement she feels at the misapplication of traditional critical terms to her novels, indicate this. Joyce's parodic exploitation of novel styles in *Ulysses* is perhaps the funniest exploration of this preoccupation. Inevitably language and the nature of human discourse will become a major theme for the modernist novelist (and playwright), for to understand the modern mind we need to understand the medium in which this mind exists – language. Woolf's view that the novel may become more 'poetic', can perhaps best be seen in this context.

Not surprisingly, therefore, Henry James and Proust stand on the threshold of the new realms which the novel will explore in the twentieth century. Both were acutely aware that they were no longer in a position to write the kind of novels that the nineteenth-century novel tradition was offering them, and were thus forced to reappraise the novelist's activity (and therefore his relationship to his reader). They mapped out regions into which Joyce, Woolf and Beckett, among others, were to venture, and to bring back for us such testaments of the modernist spirit as *Ulysses*, *The Waves* and the *Trilogy*; novels we should read, a little better to read ourselves.

## Pound's *Hugh Selwyn Mauberley*

Ezra Pound's *Hugh Selwyn Mauberley*, published in June 1920, was one of the first major modernist achievements. In its eighteen sections of between eight and thirty-seven lines Pound compressed his view of contemporary English culture. Not only this, but he also presented three versions of poetic responsibility, the conventional, and those of Mauberley and the E.P. who is commemorated in the first poem. As K. K. Ruthven puts it in his illuminating commentary *A Guide to Ezra Pound's 'Personae'* (1969), the poem depends on 'its subtle investigation of the intricate relationship between Pound, E.P. and Mauberley.'

The opening 'Ode' presents E.P. only to remove him somewhat

peremptorily from the literary scene. It has often been quoted and anthologized, though taken on its own it would imply a negation not present in the poem as a whole. The misguided American, 'born in a half-savage country, out of date', has left the scene, having failed in his irrelevant ambition 'to resuscitate the dead art of poetry'. The solemnity of the tone is remarkably poised: the reader is held at a distance.

The reference to 'the march of events', the journalistic cliché marked off in Jamesian quotation marks, leads into the next two sections. Clearly the departed poet was unable to fulfil the demands of the age, but since these were for 'a mould in plaster/Made with no loss of time' the failure is not his. The world has changed for the worse: 'Caliban casts out Ariel' – though the quatrains of this third section lack the elegance and bite which would render them fully effective. The following sections, on the war, achieve real authority:

> Daring as before, wastage as never before.
> Young blood and high blood,
> fair cheek, and fine bodies;
>
> fortitude as never before
>
> frankness as never before,
> disillusions as never told in the old days,
> hysterias, trench confessions,
> laughter out of dead bellies.

The unfeeling plurals here enact the commonplaceness of the disasters to humanity and the final unnerving suggestion ('laughter out of dead bellies') crystallizes the feeling of perversion and macabre horror. The apparent simplicity of the fifth section brings the poem to its first climax:

> There died a myriad,
> And of the best, among them,
> For an old bitch gone in the teeth,
> For a botched civilization,

> Charm, smiling at the good mouth,
> Quick eyes gone under earth's lid,
>
> For two gross of broken statues,
> For a few thousand battered books.

The diction, with its movement from the dignity of 'myriad' to the coarseness of 'bitch', and the rhythm, so skilfully held back for the anti-climactic ending of the last stanza, fuse into an achieved bitterness of tone that is not merely personal.

The next seven sections present aspects of English culture to suggest how the tradition had come to be so empty. The Victorian period is crystallized into the 'yeux glauques' of a Pre-Raphaelite stunner. Although the opening lines –

> Gladstone was still respected
> When John Ruskin produced
> 'King's Treasuries'; Swinburne
> And Rossetti still abused –

imply that respect for Gladstone, and by implication Ruskin, is no longer possible, Swinburne and Rossetti hardly emerge as heroes. They are associated with the eyes of a Burne-Jones beggar-maid,

> Thin like brook-water,
> With a vacant gaze.

The section ends with witty rhyme and juxtaposition of ideas:

> Bewildered that a world
> Shows no surprise
> At her last maquero's
> Adulteries.

The combination of innocence and sophistication is neatly suggested, as is the change of manners which made the scandals of the Victorian era unremarkable to the worldlier Georgians. The exotic word 'maquero' suggests the aura with which Rossetti and his admirers liked to surround themselves, while the single word

'Adulteries' is another well managed anti-climax when some more romantic synonym is expected. The nineties as recalled by M. Verog in the next section again suggest a culture hollow at the core. The Dantean title only underlies the triviality of Yeats's 'Tragic Generation'. In this section, though, the information is conveyed somewhat flatly – except perhaps in the line 'Dowson found harlots cheaper than hotels.' This is even more succinct than Yeats's 'Sober he would look at no other woman, it was said, but, drunk, desired whatever woman chance brought, clean or dirty' in the *Autobiographies*.

The five portraits that follow contribute to the sense of rootlessness, lack of valid purpose. Brennbaum's elegance is a race-denying mask. Mr Nixon's literary success is based on a cynical calculation of career prospects. 'The stylist' has retired to Nature only to achieve the all-too-material. The woman who might, according to Remy de Gourmont's view of women, be expected to continue the sensual tradition, is 'in Ealing/With the most bank-clerkly of Englishmen', and has been cut down to her social size. Finally the Lady Valentine in her 'stuffed-satin drawing-room' is a patron of the arts with her own dubious reasons:

> A hook to catch the Lady Jane's attention,
> A modulation towards the theatre,
> Also, in the case of revolution,
> A possible friend and comforter.

The contrast between Dr Johnson's Fleet Street and that of 1920 is sharply pointed:

> Beside this thoroughfare
> The sale of half-hose has
> Long since superseded the cultivation
> Of Pierian roses.

Perhaps the pointing is too sharp, the contrast too simple. If we substitute Grub Street for Fleet Street we are made aware of the more complex and uncomfortable realities of cultural history.

The section ends with the beautiful 'Envoi':

> Go, dumb-born book,
> Tell her that sang me once that song of Lawes:
> Hadst thou but song
> As thou hast subjects known,
> Then were there cause in thee that should condone
> Even my faults that heavy upon me lie,
> And build her glories their longevity.

The musical eloquence of this derives from the tradition of Waller but acquires poignancy from its placing amid the ironic quatrains of the 'modern' style of the rest of the poem, and from the implication that such beauty is only attainable as a deliberate reversion to an earlier style. The 'Envoi' is a successful poem both in its own terms and in those of the tradition it derives from. It moves with grace through its affirmation of the power of art – 'I would bid them live/As roses might, in magic amber laid' – to a final plain declaration:

> Tell her that goes
> With song upon her lips
> But sings not out the song, nor knows
> The maker of it, some other mouth,
> May be as fair as hers,
> Might, in new ages, gain her worshippers,
> When our two dusts with Waller's shall be laid,
> Sifting on siftings, in oblivion,
> Till change hath broken down
> All things save beauty alone.

The suggestion by Donald Davie in the Pelican *The Modern Age* that we should see this section as directly addressed to the Spirit of England is convincing. The poem as a whole, indeed, was described by Pound in a footnote to the first American edition as 'distinctly a farewell to London'. The farewell includes Pound's energetic repudiation of the various falsenesses of the cultural life as he had experienced it, but here he pays eloquent tribute to the all-but-extinguished tradition of English poetry in which he shows himself to be an accomplished participator. The final, rather awkward, line: 'All things save beauty alone' rests on Pound's single enduring value – a spirit to be distinguished from the 'two gross of broken statues' to which it has become reduced.

After this poignant climax, the sequence of poems called 'Mauberly 1920' reverts to a detached·tone and an ironic manner, to survey the career of another poet, who, like E.P., had been a follower of Flaubert's aesthetic emphasis. But in this case a distinction is suggested. This is along lines similar to those in T. S. Eliot's 'Arnold and Pater' (1930), between 'the right practice of "art for art's sake" ... the devotion of Flaubert or Henry James' and the attempt to make a religion of art at the expense of life. Hugh Selwyn Mauberley, whose elegant name suggests the stance of a dandy, turns to the medallion:

> his art, but an art
> in profile.

The second and third sections, the longest in the poem, give an account of Mauberley's life over the three years E.P. devoted to the attempted resuscitation of 'the dead art/Of poetry'. This is the part of the poem referred to by Pound in a letter of July 1922 to Felix Schelling:

> (Of course I'm no more Mauberley than Eliot is Prufrock. Mais passons). Mauberley is a mere surface. Again a study in form, an attempt to condense the James novel. Meliora speramus.

Hugh Kenner has quoted a passage from *The Ambassadors* about Strether's 'phantasmagoria' to emphasize the relationship. This is clearly James's world of wealth and waste, in which the fastidious aesthete shrinks from ugliness only to find that he has excluded life itself. The quatrains drift among the dots of unfinished sentences as Mauberley's life drifts towards extinction. By the time he has a sieve to sift value from experience it is too late: the instrument has become a seismograph, recording the shades of reality with scientific detachment. His devotion to a narrow aestheticism left him only a retrospective sense of the erotic passion he had failed to notice at the time. A feeling of frustration and emptiness is conveyed by the 'Mouths biting empty air' which serve as his negative 'epilogues'.

'The Age Demanded' places Mauberley's private story in its public context. The poet's dilemma is rendered clearly, with no overt judgment:

> The glow of porcelain
> Brought no reforming sense
> To his perception
> Of the social inconsequence.

The last word suggests Mauberley's refusal to accept the cliché 'social consequence', his immersion in the experiences of art. Nevertheless, this art is not enough for him:

> The coral island, the iron-coloured sand
> Burst in upon the porcelain reverie:
> Impetuous troubling
> Of his imagery

The rhyme enforces the irony; the poet is so completely steeped in his art that the most troublesome aspect of his dissatisfaction is its effect not on his life but his imagery; he cannot himself make the link. He becomes more and more introverted and isolated, achieving an 'Olympian *apathein*'. Pound's sympathy for his creation comes out in the unexpected beauty of the language describing his final withdrawal:

> Left him delighted with the imaginary
> Audition of the phantasmal sea-surge...

And the final quatrain directs its irony in two directions:

> Non-esteem of self-styled 'his betters'
> Leading, as he well knew,
> To his final
> Exclusion from the world of letters.

The fourth section allows Mauberley to drift right away from European culture to the romantic 'Moluccas', the fabled Malay spice-islands. Here he gradually dwindles – the poetry enacts this with delicacy – into an epitaph:

> 'I was
> And I no more exist;
> Here drifted
> An hedonist.'

He has composed a suitably chaste form of words to convey the sense of the failure of his hedonism to give value to life. The word is chosen to acknowledge Mauberley's place in the tradition of Pater's Conclusion to *The Renaissance* ('For our one chance lies in expanding that interval, in getting as many pulsations as possible into the given time'), and to suggest the emptiness of the creed. It implies the distinction between a true devotion to beauty as a social value and a mere self-involved aestheticism. The art of Mauberley is generally said to be directly represented in 'Medallion', with which the whole poem ends. We are given a portrait in which the subject, a woman, is completely transformed into art – or, perhaps, into science:

> The face – oval beneath the glaze,
> Bright in its suave bounding-line, as
> Beneath half-watt rays,
> The eyes turn topaz.

The final emphasis is on the woman's eyes, but far from having any expressive power these have now become the enigmatic reflectors of the rays to which they are exposed. No Botticellian eroticism here: Anadyomene is seen only in the 'opening/Pages of Reinach', as frontispiece to a scholarly work. Art has been absorbed into the academic, the aesthetic, the non-vital. The tradition of Waller is not taken up by the modern aesthete, secluded in his alienation.

What marks out Pound's attitude is the force of his protest against this situation despite his sense of its attractions; as he wrote in his letter to Felix Schelling:

> It's all rubbish to pretend that art isn't didactic. A revelation is always didactic. Only the aesthetes since 1880 have pretended the contrary, and they aren't a very sturdy lot.
>
> Art can't offer a patent medicine. A failure to dissociate that from a profounder didacticism has led to the error of 'aesthete's' critique.

*Hugh Selwyn Mauberley* offers itself, then, as a revelation, the embodiment of 'a profounder didacticism'. The claim, character-istic of modernist art, is a large one. The brevity of the poem does not detract from this. Indeed, the appeal for the modernist of a method which avoids lengthy commentary and explicitness is partly that it enables him to compress much into little. Of course, this is not necessarily the reader's experience. In his effort to see the work as a whole, there may be as much expenditure of time, and more of concentration, than in reading a larger, more explicit work. The application of the epigraph from the third-century Carthaginian poet Nemesianus, 'Vocat aestus in umbram' (heat calls into shade) is perhaps a case in point. By the end of our reading, 'aestus' has been given a good deal of substance for social and cultural history, and the 'umbra' has taken on a less comforting suggestion as Mauberley finally withdraws into it. For good or ill, Pound was never to respond to that particular call. Eliot praised the poem in his Introduction to the *Selected Poems of Ezra Pound* (1928):

> It is compact of the experience of a certain man in a certain place at a certain time; and it is also a document of an epoch; it is genuine tragedy and comedy; and it is, in the best sense of Arnold's worn phrase, a 'criticism of life'.

At the very least *Hugh Selwyn Mauberley*, in its inclusiveness, its flexibility of tone, and its belief in the power of art, is a vital and entertaining expression of the modernist spirit in poetry.

## Joyce's *Ulysses*, by Jeremy Lane

Despite or because of being 'usylessly unreadable' (its author's own humorously anagrammatical judgment in the even less scrutable *Finnegans Wake*), Joyce's *Ulysses* has become, for the English-speaking peoples at least, a prime example of the modern in literature. Though now over fifty years old (first published in February 1922) it remains a potent image of modernity in fiction, despite our age of swiftly and, so it is claimed, radically changing literary fashions. An *image* of modernity – for the reputation of *Ulysses* is, like most reputations, largely the fruit of ignorance, in particular a kind of schooled ignorance. The book is a staple of the academic industry, a 'text' more discussed and 'interpreted' than read, whose gargantuan bulk has over the years been further increased – distended, some might say – by the eager attentions of critic and cryptologist. Mouthful after mouthful of analysis and exegesis has been fed into *Ulysses*, which now looms massively over the landscape of twentieth-century literature and has consequently come to be viewed by later writers (and readers too) as an obstacle to be overcome or avoided as much as a challenge to be welcomed. Is it a work of nihilism, a literary *cul-de-sac*, or a work of infinite promise, the gateway to a new conception of the art of fiction? Throughout its history *Ulysses* has stimulated contradictory responses and its capacity to do so is perhaps the surest indication of its true modernity.

For *Ulysses* is an exemplar of Modernism in its uncompromising determination to found itself upon contradiction and paradox. Joyce persistently refuses recourse to structures and securities which, though they have sustained literature in the past, he feels to lack validity for the present. His fiction raises questions to which there can be no actual solution, although since, as Wittgenstein noted, any question necessarily implies the possibility of an answer, *possible* solutions, various and contradictory, remain. Paradox then is the very stuff of *Ulysses*, a book which, more perhaps than any, save its own successor *Finnegans Wake*, relies upon other books and other ways of writing, and yet is also a book like no other – a novel so uncommon that it poses at the outset the question whether it may be termed a 'novel' at all, seeming as it does to lack almost all the qualities of the novel as it is generally understood, having virtually no story, no plot, almost no action, little characterization in the usual sense, no real adventure or romantic interest, no moral values or significant philosophy to impart. Broadly speaking (which, in the case of *Ulysses*, is to speak most narrowly) the novel concerns the thoughts, experiences, and above all the encounter of two men during a single day, 16 June 1904, in Dublin – a day marked by nothing outwardly notable, a day of no apparent historical significance, nor even of any clear personal significance to the protagonists themselves. Leopold Bloom, a Dublin Jew, married with a daughter (a son having died in infancy), advertisement-canvasser for a newspaper, is one of these men – in character and role mild and middling, middle-aged, middle-class, middle-brow, of mittel-European extraction, *l'homme sensuel moyen*. The other is a figure previously encountered as the 'hero' of Joyce's novel, *A Portrait of the Artist as a Young Man*, Stephen Dedalus, would-be writer, aesthete and intellectual, enjoying a certain notoriety in the provincial society of Edwardian Dublin. (The surname Dedalus, in this fiction where words and especially names count for so much, goes a fair way towards characterizing him – bizarre, Hellenic, faintly pretentious, it contrasts in multiple respects with Bloom.) A third person, Molly, the adulterous Mrs Bloom, who plays an importantly different, background role, makes up the novel's profane trinity of major characters.

The novel gives an account, at what is by any conventional inordinate length, of the movements, physical and psychological, of the two men as they pass the day – a day outwardly distinguished merely by their encounter and, consequently, by the sober and kindly Bloom's rescue of Stephen after a drunken affray, a Samaritan act for which he gets little thanks. Subsequently Bloom invites Stephen back to his home, where he dispenses cups of cocoa and the two converse desultorily, while Molly is sleeping upstairs.

Stephen leaves in the early hours of the morning and Bloom goes to bed and to sleep. So far as it is a narrative of 'Bloomsday', *Ulysses* ends there, but there is a further episode, the famous monologue by Molly Bloom – matutinal musings expressing essential femininity (at least according to Joyce's prescription), marked by a gossipy interest in others, an earthy interest in the functions, sexual and excretory, of the human body, and an absence of punctuation. So much, or nearly, for the narrative content of *Ulysses*. Such a description says nothing however about its form and this is a fatal omission concerning a work in which forms and content are indivisible, where the 'how' of expression and style cannot be meaningfully detached from the 'what' of content and substance. Formally, the novel begins in a relatively straightforward manner, but rapidly develops into a more and more stylistically and verbally complex and changeable fiction, incorporating a plethora of rhetorical and literary forms. Many who have never in fact read *Ulysses* have heard of the episode set in the Maternity Hospital, where the foetal growth of a newborn baby is recorded analogically by means of virtuoso pastiches of various styles of English throughout literary history, from early English alliterative to American twentieth-century hot gospel. The fame of the 'Aeolus' episode, where newspaper 'headlines' interrupt the text (a device much imitated by later writers, from Dos Passos on), or of the 'Circe' episode, the brothel scene cast in the form of an expressionist drama, has reached those who have never opened the book. Again paradox asserts itself: such a diversity and multiplicity of forms and styles and such a sheer quantity and variety of language are employed by a writer who, in terms of content, of substance, appears to have nothing, or virtually nothing, to say.

One may claim that such a paradox is of the essence of this fiction however, for *Ulysses* is a work which strives to say everything and nothing, both 'yes' and 'no' simultaneously. While its conclusion is affirmative, its course is a series of negations – and course and conclusion cannot be separated. Molly, the Penelope of this latter-day *Odyssey*, opens and closes her great monologue, her enormous mouth, with the word 'Yes', yet she has in the course of the narrative denied her husband in her adulterous liaison with her lover Blazes Boylan. The cuckolded Bloom, a modern Everyman but also Odysseus, Noman, a nobody whose diary *Ulysses*, as Bloomsday, partly is, concludes in abnegation, in a self-denial which is however an ultimate acceptance. Stephen is most consciously and consistently a negator, having refused his mother's deathbed request to pray for her, having rejected church, country, and family (the threefold denial promised in the *Portrait*), and rejecting in the course of Bloomsday the suspect friendship of the 'archmocker' Mulligan. Finally he declines Bloom's overtures too (the invitation to stay the night, and, more speculatively, to give Molly Italian and singing lessons and Bloom himself intellectual conversation). Yet he has nevertheless in some sense, however passive, accepted the help and company of the other man and that acceptance carries in itself, if nothing else, at least the possibility of some kind of affirmation – Stephen's eventual self-affirmation as an artist (which is a kind of self-denial), the creation of a work of art, even such a work as *Ulysses*. We have to recognize that every affirmation includes negation, for in this fiction the course cannot be divorced from the conclusion. In fact there can be no distinct conclusion, as the double ending of *Ulysses*, with its cyclical implications, makes clear. The novel 'ends' twice, each time indeterminately: once as narrative, fictional history, Bloomsday, with the cryptic final question of the 'Ithaca' episode – 'Where?' (answered in certain editions by an ovular dot, an outsize full stop, truly periodic); once as a verbal construct, as a book, with Molly's final and initial 'Yes', in whose end is perpetually a beginning. This dual finality prevents conclusiveness, the certainty that 'there it is, there we have it'.

This questioning reaches the deepest levels, demanding the consideration of problems of knowing and being with which religion and philosophy have traditionally concerned themselves. But the enquiry is made in the terms, not of religion or philosophy, but of *fiction* – generally in terms of literature and especially in terms of narrative. *Ulysses* manifests pre-eminently the self-consciousness characteristic of modernist literature. Sceptical of the truth of all else, its attention must rest initially and ultimately upon itself, upon its own paradoxical actuality as fiction, a reality which is not true, a truth which is not reality. This self-consciousness is quite distinct from the Romantic conception of the transcendental Self (though it finds its derivation there) and involves, not the Romantic assertion of an identity between self and world, but on the contrary the recognition of a disparity, a disparity contained however within an integer, the work of art itself. *Ulysses* thus insists, first and last, upon its status and quality as artifact and fiction.

However, the critical reader needs to have some idea of the novel as a product of history as well as an autonomous creation. He wants to acknowledge the particular work as a self-sufficient entity but also as a witness to its time and place, and thus to the movements of sensibility that have led up to and away from it. It is Joyce's achievement to have recognized and made evident in *Ulysses* that the two elements, fiction and history, are both inalienable and yet intransigently hostile. The form which seeks to combine them, the novel, *this* novel, cannot therefore presume to effect their synthesis. The attempt to comprehend both elements is thus marked evidently and finally by neither success nor failure, which is to say that it is characterized implicitly by both – success in failure, failure in success. *Ulysses* recounts a portion of history and in doing so must fail to tell a story in the conventional sense, the 'story' which supplies a form and finality to existence. *Ulysses*, as we have seen, 'ends' twice, once for Bloom and this day (one story, one history), once for his wife (and hers is the story of a lifetime). It begins twice too, once for Stephen (and the reader) and once again, at the beginning of the fourth chapter, for Bloom. Potentially it might begin and end an infinite number of times, as many times as there are individual histories. This plurality is a negation of both History and Story, the single account which, whether supposedly factual or fictional, presumes to tell all there is to be told. Yet the fiction is necessarily composed of the historical and the narrative. *Ulysses* then does not easily or conclusively submit to history (either the documentary history intrinsic to its subject-matter, the Dublin *demos* at a particular date, or the literary and cultural history which pervades its form). Nor does it easily or conclusively triumph over history, as a strictly aesthetic determination like Stephen's would have it do, creating a 'story' which is its own negation, pure and timeless. It remains the battleground on which the perpetual and insoluble conflict between fiction and history is waged.

This conflict may be seen reflected in the rivalry between aesthetic ideas, ideas which are themselves products of historical process but also the producers of those extraordinary manifestations of the human spirit which stand in some sense out of time, beyond the sweep of history – manifestations we are apt to call 'works of art'. *Ulysses*, recognizing and embodying the conflict, also reflects the rivalry, which may generally be described as that between a realistic or mimetic and an irrealistic or (in a strict sense) poetic conception of art. In both local and wider contexts of literary tradition the reaction of *Ulysses* is double. Locally, the novel is a response to both of the quarrelling voices of nineteenth-century culture – the voice of the Realist, claiming art to be essentially mimesis, and the voice of the Symbolist or Aesthete, vaunting art as mystery or artifice. *Ulysses* has been viewed as the *ne plus ultra* of Naturalism, out-documenting Zola, but also as the most extensive and elaborate of Symbolist poems. Each of these readings is valid, but only if taken in relation to the other, for the novel is the' site of their interaction and negotiation. It is precisely in the relation between these basically incompatible readings that the experience of *Ulysses* consists. That relation is personified dramatically in the narrative through the process of encounter undergone by Stephen and Bloom, and thematically in the third person of the Ulyssean trinity, the flesh made word, Molly Bloom. In its structure and subject-matter *Ulysses*, through its conjunction of opposing modes (which historically have become disjoined), operates a critique of each upon the other in such a way that the limitations but also the necessity of both are affirmed.

The critique is not however restricted to the local arena, the dispute between Naturalism and Symbolism, for example. *Ulysses* is far more ambitious, seeking to include within its 'terms of reference' – a reference which is always critical and usually strongly parodic – as many modes of literary discourse and representation as possible. It comprises a conscious response not only to local orthodoxies but, much further, to the whole tradition of western European literature, from Homer onwards. Of course this response cannot be inclusive. Joyce is perfectly aware that the writer cannot hope to contain the culture of a civilization within the covers of a single book. But he is also aware that the ambition to do so, doomed to failure, is nevertheless a condition of the novel's creation. It is because this culture has lost its integrity and strength that the writer is compelled to attempt its 'reintegration' in the only terms possible, those of fiction. In other words, there is no longer an integrating faith, a creative belief in the world's wholeness, to which the writer may, in the fullest sense, subscribe. Instead there is an integrating fiction, the novel which amasses a multifarious and seemingly inchoate world, crammed with phenomena of whose significance there is no assurance, and which asserts itself to be fundamentally and superficially a matter of language, of words, words, words. Faith itself may be defined as substantive fiction, so that, deprived of faith, richly furnished with doubt, the writer is left with a fiction that is insubstantive, whose power to give substance to an idea is questioned, together with the corresponding power to idealize the substantial world. The modernist writer is therefore compelled to construct, consciously, a multiple analogy between his fiction and others which, though in their own terms true, must remain for him essentially fictitious. The most notable of these other fictions is, of course, the *Odyssey* of Homer; but *Ulysses* is a parodic and plural analogy, relating itself through form and style, through language, to various forms of *poesis*, themselves exposed thereby as fictions, as modes of conceiving and constructing the world.

Two principal and contrary modes are personified in the two

major protagonists of *Ulysses*. In Bloom and in a major aspect of the narrative (for one should remember that the principal figures in *Ulysses* largely narrate their world as well as acting it) the order of Realism, of the mimetic adoption of external and empirically apprehensible reality, is given the fullest expression. Defoe's Crusoe and Moll Flanders, man and woman of the world, of possessions, of domestic faith, of petit-bourgeois culture, are 'heroically' pictured in Joyce's Mr and Mrs Bloom, and their representation gives *Ulysses* title as a novel. Yet this representation is continually subject to parody and distortion, to the violations of fiction, notably in the long 'Circe' episode, the phantasmagoria of the brothel scene, in which the order of Realism and its hero, Bloom, suffer the tyrannies of fantasy. It may be claimed that ultimately reality (in the generally accepted sense) prevails, that eventually, with Bloom and Stephen, we return, rescuer and rescued, from a world of weirdness (of 'wordness') to the world we habitually think we know. This, broadly, has been the view of those critics who wish to make a traditional, orthodox novel out of *Ulysses*. Yet, in the episode which immediately succeeds 'Circe', common reality remains the subject of a formal interpretation, a modulation, which is far from straightforward. Here banality surely mocks itself as the tired triteness of 'Eumaeus' exposes ordinary, habitual 'realization' to parody. And while there may be a *nostos* for Bloom, a return to the reality of home and wife, that too is qualified by the abstractive mode of the penultimate chapter, its catechistical form and forensic style. For Stephen moreover there is no immediate or, as it were, straightforward return. His must be a passage back by means of a movement forward, out into the Dublin night with its intimation of dawn, to reality in and through the fiction, *Ulysses* itself – the imaginative work which proposes itself as his possibility, the creation in which he may potentially realize himself in another.

Stephen himself, in contrast to the Blooms, personifies the order of Romanticism, in which the self and subject, not the world and object, is the principal factor. Here the figure of Blake, whom Stephen invokes at key moments, is exemplary, for in Blake the

Romantic destruction of the conventional, classical order and the corresponding assertion of a personally defined but universally defining cosmos is figured. Significantly, a Blakean phrase describes Stephen's most dramatic act of destruction –

(He lifts his ashplant high with both hands and smashes the chandelier. Time's livid final flame leaps and, in the following darkness, ruin of all space, shattered glass and toppling masonry.)

But in banal actuality all that Stephen's cosmic destructiveness has amounted to is the breaking of a lamp-chimney and the denting of its shade. Romantic pretension, here and elsewhere throughout the novel, is debunked by its incongruous juxtaposition with prosaic reality. The pretension is not however negligible, because it is necessitated by Stephen's situation. As a would-be artist and an extraordinarily sensitive young man, whose self-concern is after all a measure of his sensibility, he is quite aware that he lacks the assurance sustaining both classical and realist writers, the confidence that the writer shares with his readers a sense of what is significant in human experience. That loss of assurance is the paradoxically negative creation of the Romantic spirit and Stephen, sharing in the loss, is bound, especially as an intending creator, to share in its source. Responsibility to the individual self, independent of conventionally ordered assumptions about reality, is the inescapable legacy of Romanticism which Stephen is obliged to accept. But the pretended powers of the Self, concomitantly asserted by the Romantic, Stephen is neither compelled nor, eventually, able to claim. It is in the gradual realization of this incapacity, which is also a liberty, that Stephen's experience within the narrative of *Ulysses* importantly consists. It is through the awareness of this incapacity and of the possibilities it permits that the reader discovers in *Ulysses*, claustrophobic as its world appears to be, a kind of liberation.

Thus it is that the later derivatives of the Classic-Romantic conflict, the various literary movements of the nineteenth century which represent attempts to solve, one way or the other, the dilemma that conflict poses, also come under the critical gaze of *Ulysses*. The fallacy of Aestheticism, the tendency to subjugate life to Art, is sharply criticized in Stephen and the 'artistic' circle in which, initially, he moves (Mulligan's hellenic fraternity, the *cénacle* of the Library scene). The principle of *l'art pour l'art* appeals to Stephen, recently back from Paris, since it erects a kind of godless theology of Art in opposition to the overbearing secularism of humanistic Realism, but it is demonstrated by the novel to be an inadequate solution. The converse fallacy of Realism, the tendency to subjugate art to Life, is no less thoroughly, though perhaps, in the nature of things, more indulgently criticized in Bloom and the naturalistic mode he represents. If the theologically minded self-proclaimed 'freethinker' Stephen is exposed, so too is the secularly ecumenical Bloom. The multiple of both (with the third element, Molly), the novel, presents a conjunction of opposing modes which prevents prescription according to either alone. The secular and rationalistic world view is combined, but not synthesized, with the theological and sacramental, and the limitations of both are made apparent. The conception of a realistic world, a present, concrete, and apprehensible actuality is conjoined with that of an ideal world, absent, essential, mediated through allusion and symbol. Neither is permitted hegemony, since each is understood to depend upon the other. The secular view, which produces the world of buttons and breakfast (the world in which Bloom for the most part has his being), the world of what is normally taken for reality, is itself seen to be a kind of fiction. The sacramental view, which produces what is normally assumed to be the transcendental world, the 'other-worldly', the world of myth, of poetry, of portents and symbols (the world in which Stephen for the most part seeks to move) is also seen to be a fiction, but attaining in that self-consciousness an essential, though quite 'other' reality.

We are led to recognize that the creative act – observing and recording the world in relation to the self – is an act of choice. Perspective, the modernist acknowledges, necessitates partiality. As the Romantics understood, viewing and imitating the world are not merely passive, but active and constructive processes. Perception is also prescription: to interpret is in an important sense to create. But, without the security of an overall substantive fiction, a faith and its accompanying *mythos*, there can be no assurance for the modernist writer that his perceptions and interpretations are valid and true. The writer is unable to adopt any particular, pre-scribed interpretation and yet unable to refuse his particular per-ception. He must search for meaning without the prior assurance that any meaning may be found. That quest is a process of choosing and integrating the choices made, the process which constructs the fiction, *Ulysses*, itself. This 'novel' seeks therefore to evade the extrinsic limitations of genre. For doubt to be affirmed, all must be doubted, qualified, undermined, above all the generic modes of dis-course and narrative representation in which assumptions lie most cunningly concealed. Of course we call *Ulysses* a novel, adopting the unexceptionable Forsterian definition of it as 'a fiction in prose of a certain extent' – in this case extended, like Milton's Satan, 'long and large'. If we view the novel as the most capacious form of fiction-making yet devised, a kind of Autolycus' bag in which a potentially illimitable quantity of material, all in a sense the stuff of language, can be packed, then we may call *Ulysses* a novel. But it has equal claims to be called a poem, and we must conclude that in the end it resists the usual generic definitions. In Harry Levin's famous phrase, it is 'the novel to end all novels'.

Perhaps, therefore, it is helpful to describe *Ulysses* as a 'fiction' (a term significantly in vogue with modernists), in order to emphasize its nature as process as well as its status as product. Such a description may also help to counter the prevailing idea of the novel as 'mythical' or 'mythological', terms which, unqualified, are dangerously misleading. *Ulysses* is a work, not of mythopoeia, but of fiction: not an attempt to recreate in modern terms the myth of Odysseus, of voyage and return, even of the filial and paternal quest, so much as a basic questioning of the very possibility of mythic vision for modern man. It is a playfully desperate utilization rather than acceptance of myth, which involves, not taking a mythic world for granted but taking it, so to speak, 'in for questioning'. For myth is a fiction, a story, consonant with and expressive of faith – a faith, that is, infused with substance – and we have seen that *Ulysses* denies such faith and, correspondingly, lacks such substance. The 'substance' of *Ulysses* is words, language itself, in which the whole complex, conflict-ridden relation between substantial and essential, actual and ideal, concrete and abstract, is contained.

The fictional work has always in principle contained this duality, being an imaginative act and a material product, a mental reality evoking, however indirectly, a physical world. But previous fiction, whether classically or Romantically, realistically or symbolistically based, was largely able to synthesize the two worlds, one way or the other, and so bring them into concordance. The modernist work's foundation on doubt, and the peculiar degree of self-consciousness which this enforces, requires the acknowledgement of its dual status as an imaginative act in which both subjective and objective reality are realized to be necessarily conjunct and inextricably related, but by no means consonant. Unable to ignore or evade or transcend this duality, in ways formerly possible, the fiction attempts to probe its implications to the uttermost. It seeks ambitiously the comprehension of duality, the containment of paradox, antithesis, contradiction – a containment which demands the reformulation of 'content', whereby the traditionally assumed dichotomy of content and form is annihilated, while the distinction between them is maintained. The integration of form and content, of diverse style and subject-matter, compels duality and its comprehension: the two are not identified with one another (the Mabbott Street brothel does not *equal* either Circe's cave or an Expressionist drama), but they are revealed to be indivisible. *Ulysses* is the unstable compound of its content and form, carrying a burden of circumstantial reality, the day-to-dayness of Dublin, whose heaviness is equalled only by the capacity of its formal virtuosity to juggle with it almost in defiance of gravity. The novel is grounded, bogged, some might feel, in the contingent and phenomenal, the fact-filled, encyclopaedic account of the minutiae of small-city life. But this ground is mined, more and more thoroughly as the 'narrative' proceeds. *Ulysses* has neither the imperturbable solidity of the realistic narrative nor the ethereality of the symbolic fiction, but the disturbing, disorienting, yet strangely exhilarating quality of a medium at once consistent and mobile, whose elements, form and content, are continually attracting and repulsing one another, merging and separating.

'I called you naughty boy because I do not like that other world. Please tell what is the real meaning of that word.' So writes Martha Clifford, Bloom's postal 'mistress', to her correspondent, and the significantly accidental misliteration of 'word' to 'world', together with the plea for 'real meaning' reflects in ridiculous miniature the creative confusion and quest embodied in *Ulysses* as a whole. For, in *Ulysses*, Joyce implicitly and creatively acknow-ledges the relation of connection and disjunction operating between language and reality, word and world, to be the fundamental condition of fiction. The novel thus admits the dual, contradictory, and equal claims of both chance and necessity inherent in its medium and material, language. The world must be lived in – there is nowhere else – yet language, the enactment of consciousness, sets man outside the world. The fiction, rejecting the totalitarian claims of both idealism and materialism, affirms itself as inseparable and yet distinct from the phenomenal world, admitting the inter-reliance and rivalry between the world as Idea (noumenon, symbol, artifact) and the world as Will or Being (phenomenon, thing, fact). So the fiction, the admission of both chance and necessity, is, like life, no simple, once-and-for-all matter but a perpetual process, an endless choosing, a continual research and reconsideration. Yet it is also, in the sense that it demands an initial, vital commitment, in principle a movement of release and liberation, even of abandon. It is the process we experience enacted in the narrative of *Ulysses*, the odyssey and *nostos* of Bloom, Stephen's remorseful self-scrutiny and final departure, Molly's remorseless recollection and her initial and final yeasaying. It is the fiction itself: the acceptance of chance and necessity, of contingent but inescapable experience, but also the affirmation of choice, the attempt at comprehension, perpetually thwarted and perpetually renewed. Ultimately the vision of *Ulysses* is, I believe, comic, with that fundamentally ironic strain of comedy which characterizes a great proportion of modernist literature, the works, for example, of Proust, Musil, Mann, and Kafka. Joyce's is a comedy not divine, ending, like Dante's, in the vision of a God in whose will is our peace, but human all-too-human, 'ending' in acquiescence and affirmation of a different kind – in Molly's 'yes I will Yes', an acquiescence in the world's will, its necessity and contingency, and an affirmation of human wilfulness, the life and fiction each man is forced and free to choose.

## D. H. Lawrence and Modernism

Lawrence's relationship to Modernism is complex. He was a deliberate innovator in his method as a novelist, and yet he had scant respect for either the modernists or the predecessors whom they particularly admired, giving his respect to earlier traditional English novelists like George Eliot and Hardy. In 'Surgery for the Novel – or a Bomb?' in 1923, for example, he ridiculed the self-consciousness of Proust, Joyce and Dorothy Richardson:

> So there you have the 'serious' novel, dying in a very long-drawn-out fourteen-volume death-agony, and absorbedly, childishly interested in the phenomenon. 'Did I feel a twinge in my little toe, or didn't I?' asks every character of Mr. Joyce or of Miss Richardson or M. Proust. Is my aura a blend of frankincense and orange pekoe and boot-blacking, or is it myrrh and bacon-fat and Shetland tweed? The audience round the death-bed gapes for the answer. And when, in a sepulchral tone, the answer comes at length, after hundreds of pages: 'It is none of these, it is abysmal chloro-coryambasis', the audience quivers all over, and murmurs: 'That's just how I feel myself.'

This is penetrating wit, raising a fundamental point about the self-consciousness of modernist literature. And similar judgments occur through Lawrence's letters and critical writings. The 1913 essay on Thomas Mann places him in the tradition of Flaubert as a novelist preoccupied with form, and attacks that influential tradition as fatally flawed:

> Thomas Mann seems to me the last sick sufferer from the complaint of Flaubert. The latter stood away from life as from a leprosy . . .

> His expression may be very fine. But by now what he expresses is stale. I think we have learned our lesson, to be sufficiently aware of the fulsomeness of life. And even while he has a rhythm in style, yet his work has none of the rhythm of a living thing, the rise of a poppy, then the after uplift of a bud, the shedding of the calyx and the spreading wide of the petals, the falling of the flower and the pride of the seed-head. There is an unexpectedness in this such as does not come from their carefully plotted and arranged developments. Even *Madame Bovary* seems to me dead in respect to the living rhythm of the whole work. While it is there in *Macbeth* like life itself.

Modernist literature seemed to Lawrence to be in the sterile aesthetic tradition here attacked: hence his dismissive remarks about Conrad ('why this giving in before you start . . .') and Joyce ('too terribly would-be and done-on-purpose, utterly without spontaneity or real life'). Clearly Lawrence saw his own novels in a radically different light from the modernists.

Yet Lawrence was a conscious innovator. His letters of 1913 when he was working on the novel that became *The Rainbow* show this clearly. In March he wrote to Edward Garnett:

> It's all crude as yet . . . but I think it's great – so new, so really a stratum deeper than I think anybody has ever gone, in a novel. But there, you see, it's my latest. It is all analytical – quite unlike *Sons and Lovers*, not a bit visualized.

And in an often-quoted letter in June:

> I don't think the psychology is wrong; it is only that I have a different attitude to my characters, and that necessitates a different attitude in you, which you are not prepared to give.

Lawrence then, with some reservations, related his views to those of the Italian Futurist Marinetti, who had been speaking of 'an intuitive physiology of matter':

> I translate him clumsily, and his Italian is obfuscated – and I don't care about physiology of matter – but somehow – that which is physic – non-human, in humanity, is more interesting to me than the old-fashioned human element – which causes one to conceive a character in a certain moral scheme and make him consistent. The certain moral scheme is what I object to.

The whole letter is full of critical interest as Lawrence affirms his desire to go deeper than 'the old stable *ego* of the character', employing a number of a striking metaphors to convey his view, and concluding:

> Again, I say, don't look for the development of the novel to follow the lines of certain characters: the characters fall into the form of some other rhythmic form, as when one draws a fiddle-bow across a fine tray delicately sanded, the sand takes lines unknown.

Lawrence's novels at their best do embody the innovatory and exploratory qualities suggested here. In *Women in Love*, for example, Lawrence's quest for the depths of the self in his characters is unmistakable, though it may not be consistently successful. Scenes occur which cannot be accounted for according to the logic of realistic fiction, and sometimes strike the reader as almost absurd. Yet they play their necessary part in the exploration of the novel's four main characters, Gudrun and Ursula Brangwen, Gerald Crich and Rupert Birkin. Yet the word character itself may seem questionable: there is so much interest in the depths of the characters' being that they often lack credibility in their social roles. Birkin is a particularly improbable Inspector of Schools, and Gerald, for all the discussion of the mine, not much more likely as an industrialist. But on his chosen level Lawrence achieves an unmatched intensity and insight, as in the extraordinary scene in 'Water-Party' when Gudrun dances before the Highland cattle:

> Gudrun, with her arms outspread and her face uplifted, went in a strange palpitating dance towards the cattle, lifting her body towards them as if in a spell, her feet pulsing as if in some little frenzy of unconscious sensation, her arms, her wrists, her hands stretching and heaving and falling and reaching and reaching and falling, her breasts lifted and shaken towards the cattle, her throat exposed as in some voluptuous ecstasy towards them, whilst she drifted imperceptibly nearer, an uncanny white figure, towards them, carried away in its own rapt trance, ebbing in strange fluctuations upon the cattle, that waited, and ducked their heads a little in sudden contraction from her, watching all the time as if hypnotised, their bare horns branching in the clear light, as the white figure of the woman ebbed upon them, in the slow, hypnotising convulsion of the dance. She could feel them just in front of her, it was as if she had the electric pulse from their breasts running into her hands. Soon she would touch them, actually touch them. A terrible shiver of fear and pleasure went through her.

In scenes like this what is often referred to as Lawrence's poetic power achieves its full, though puzzling, effect. The strangeness of the scene, the transformation of Gudrun 'who was frightened of cattle', the spell-bound Ursula singing for the dance, the bewildered cattle 'breathing heavily with helpless fear and fascination' – these elements fuse into an unforgettable unity. But how is it to be interpreted? Is it there to tell us something about Gudrun's character? Any simple explanation seems inadequate, indeed crude. For in scenes like this, as Dr Leavis lucidly put it in *D. H. Lawrence: Novelist* (1955), we see one of the various 'ways in which Lawrence brings into the drama the forces of the psyche of which the actors' wills have no cognizance, and which, consequently, do not seem to belong to their selves'. Such scenes achieve a new depth of exploration into the nature of the self, for which the description 'symbolic' seems, as Dr Leavis says, inadequate:

> The general bearings of the incident on the potentialities of her [Gudrun's] relations with Gerald should be plain enough. To sum up the significance is another matter: the whole remarkable chapter is very complex, closely organized, and highly charged.

In passages like these Lawrence certainly achieves an effect inconceivable in the work of the Edwardians – Bennett, Wells, Galsworthy – of whom he was as critical as was Virginia Woolf. For such poetic innovations Lawrence may indeed be considered a modernist.

Yet that is not the whole of the case. There was in Lawrence an aspiration additional to that of the explorer of the psyche which is less compatible with Modernism, and that is his moral and prophetic stance. Another letter of 1913, to A. W. McLeod in April, shows this aspect of Lawrence:

> Pray to your gods for me that *Sons and Lovers* shall succeed. People should begin to take me seriously now. And I do so break my heart over England when I read the *New Machiavelli* [by H. G. Wells]. And I am so sure that only through a readjustment between men and women, and a making free and healthy of this sex, will she get out of her present atrophy. Oh, Lord, and if I don't 'subdue my art to a metaphysic', as somebody very beautifully said of Hardy, I do write because I want folk – English folk – to alter, and have more sense.

Sometimes Lawrence could be ironical about this trait in himself, as in Ursula's reprimand to Birkin in the chapter 'Moony': '*You – you* are the Sunday-school teacher – *You* – you preacher.' Nevertheless it was an essential element in his nature, and his art, giving the latter the quality of intense seriousness that Dr Leavis calls religious. In a letter to a Miss Pears about *Lady Chatterley's Lover* in April 1927 Lawrence wrote:

> It is what the world would call very improper. But you know it's not really improper – I always labour at the same thing, to make the sex relation valid and precious, instead of shameful. And this novel is the furthest I've gone.

In Lawrence, as his critical writings imply, there is a more direct moral and social intention than was characteristic of Modernism.

To state this is not necessarily to make a value judgment. But for a critic like Dr Leavis, with a strong sense of the social responsibility of art, it is a mark of Lawrence's distinction among modern writers:

> [But] the insight, the wisdom, the revived and re-educated feeling for health, that Lawrence brings are what, as our civilisation goes, we desperately need.

This direct relationship between art and society is one that Lawrence cultivated. The modernists, by contrast, are elusive about the function of art, and indirect in method. Some would see Lawrence, like E. M. Forster, Joyce Cary and Angus Wilson in a less striking way, as embodying the more responsible English tradition; at all events his achievement, and the social influence that we may surely attribute to his writings, make a contrast which helps to define the nature of Modernism. (A parallel contrast would occur in any examination of Lawrence's poetry; here too he was an innovator, but neither his theory nor his practice coincided with that of poets like Pound and Eliot.)

# 3

## Since 1930

Cultural change is a continuous process, so that it is pointless to try to tie it down to specific dates. On the other hand, the 1930s seem in retrospect to have a singular unity of preoccupation which makes them different from the preceding era. The economic breakdown and mass unemployment of the West formed a grim continuity, while the development of Fascism in Italy and Nazism in Germany initiated a process of violence which led to the invasion of Abyssinia, the Spanish Civil War, and the Second World War. In such a world, politics became a primary concern, and the new writers began to criticize the modernists for their lack of political commitment. Already in 1931, the young American critic Edmund Wilson had ended his book on recent literature, *Axël's Castle*, by saying of such writers as Eliot, Proust, Yeats and Joyce, 'though we shall continue to admire them as masters, [they] will no longer serve us as guides'. He praised their liberating influence in breaking 'out of the old mechanistic routine', but suggested that 'they have endeavoured to discourage their readers, not only with politics, but with action of any kind':

> The question begins to press us again as to whether it is possible to make a practical success of human society, and whether, if we continue to fail, a few masterpieces, however profound or noble, will be able to make life worth living even for the few people in a position to enjoy them.

The new generation of writers was much more political, generally left-wing. Especially in poetry, direct criticism of English society became frequent. Michael Roberts in the Preface to his anthology *New Signatures* in 1932, which included poems by W. H. Auden, C. Day Lewis, William Plomer and Stephen Spender, wrote of poetry being 'turned to propaganda', and Day Lewis in *A Hope for Poetry* (1934) and Louis MacNeice in *Modern Poetry* (1937) criticized the lack of political concern in the poets of the previous generation. In his autobiography, *World Within World* (1950), Spender looked back to the publication of his early poems and contrasted their revolutionary politics with the 'consciously anti-political' attitude of the previous decade. George Orwell presented the two decades in sharp antithesis in his lively essay 'Inside the Whale' in 1940:

> The typical literary man ceases to be a cultured expatriate with a leaning towards the church, and becomes an eager-minded schoolboy with a leaning towards Communism.

Orwell over-simplifies for the sake of vividness, but the contrast is valid. Men of his generation were more directly concerned with political events; the occurrences could not be ignored. Hence more committed forms of art, sometimes but not always amounting to simple propaganda: Orwell's *Animal Farm* (1945) and *Nineteen Eighty-Four* (1949) are major works of this type. Orwell himself regarded the priority of politics as something to be regretted, but nevertheless inescapable for his generation. He also felt that this situation would continue. In his late essay 'Writers and Leviathan' in 1948 he wrote:

> Of course, the invasion of literature by politics was bound to happen. It must have happened, even if the special problem of totalitarianism had never arisen, because we have developed a sort of compunction which our grandfathers did not have, an awareness of the enormous injustice and misery of the world, as a guilt-stricken feeling that one ought to be doing something about it, which makes a purely aesthetic attitude towards life impossible. No one, now, could devote himself to literature as single-mindedly as Joyce or Henry James.

This is an interesting argument, and it can certainly be stated that much of the most impressive art of the years since 1930 has had a strongly political element: examples include Sartre, Camus, Pasternak, Solzhenitsyn, Baldwin, Mailer. But it hardly applies outside literature, nor to all of that. Samuel Beckett, for instance, has proved as single-minded as Joyce in his dedication to his art. No single statement is likely to cover all recent developments in a world whose eclecticism and variety are striking.

Certainly, though, as Modernism has come to be regarded as a distinct cultural movement in the recent past, it has also come in for more direct criticisms. The most consistent hostile critic of modernist literature has been the American Yvor Winters. *Primitivism and Decadence* (1937), *Maule's Curse* (1938) and *The Anatomy of Nonsense* (1943) all question, with fervour and lucidity, the directions taken by recent literature. In the Foreword to the 1947 volume *In Defence of Reason*, which brought together the three earlier books, Winters spelled out his belief that a poem should make 'a defensible rational statement' accompanied by the appropriate emotion, his insistence on rationality challenging the modernist emphasis on non-rational inclusiveness. In England, related critical attitudes found their expression in the Fifties, especially in the group of writers associated with Robert Conquest's anthology *New Lines* (1956). A little earlier, one of the poets represented in the anthology, Donald Davie, had published *Purity of Diction in English Verse* (1952), in which he tried to explain the pleasure to be found in the non-metaphorical verse of the eighteenth century. The book was a recall to the values of lucid communication, and the discussion of the Romantics and of 'Hopkins as a Decadent Critic' ('His is the poetry and criticism of the egotistical sublime') emphasizes the value of looking back to the eighteenth century for examples of such lucidity. Davie developed these views in *Articulate Energy: An Enquiry into the Syntax of English Poetry* in 1955.

Reservations about Modernism are characteristic too of Marxist criticism, despite the burst of artistic experimentation in the Soviet Union in the years immediately after the Revolution, including the work of Mayakovsky, Blok, Pasternak and Mandelstam. The Stalinist period included an assault on 'formalism' and the establishment of the unyielding orthodoxy of Socialist Realism. Non-Russian Marxists took less rigorous lines, but their concern for society and the wide dissemination of ideas made them wary of Modernism. Alick West's *Crisis and Criticism* (1937) contained a representative discussion of Joyce. While West admired the fertile inventiveness of *Ulysses*, he also criticized its 'verbal formalism': 'We are stimulated, and then nothing comes but barren mysticism, insincerity and coldness.' A similar view was developed more fully by the best-known of Marxist critics, the Hungarian Georg Lukács, in *The Meaning of Contemporary Realism* (1957). In this book Lukács was defending 'critical realism' in the tradition of Balzac and Tolstoy, carried on as 'contemporary bourgeois realism' by Rolland, Shaw, Dreiser, Heine and Mann, against both Modernism and Socialist Realism. In 'The Ideology of Modernism' he argued that modernist writers fail to see man socially and historically, and so make his alienation, which is a social process, into an absolute. They offer a totally subjective vision, leading to 'the attenuation of reality' in Joyce, Kafka, Musil, Faulkner and Beckett, inevitably accompanied by 'dissolution of personality'. Tellingly, Lukács suggests that Kafka replaces the world by his 'angst-ridden vision of the world'. (This argument assumes the very condition the modernists question – that 'the world' is objectively real.) Kafka's *angst* is seen as 'the experience *par excellence* of modernism', which finally means 'not the enrichment but the negation of art.' This view is reaffirmed in an essay on 'Franz Kafka or Thomas Mann'. Although non-Marxist critics may be more eclectic than Lukács, they often express a view of the limitations of Modernism which is indebted to his account.

While in books like Ifor Evans' *English Literature between the Wars* (1948) and C. M. Bowra's *The Creative Experiment* (1949) it was the 'experimental' writers who were chiefly praised, it was becoming clear in the Fifties that the great modernists belonged to the past. After all, Lawrence had died in 1930, Yeats in 1939, Joyce and Virginia Woolf in 1941. True, Pound had gone on writing his *Cantos*, while Eliot had completed his *Four Quartets* only in 1944 and was trying to establish himself as a dramatist. But his plays were hardly modernist, and the influence of the innovations of the 1920s seemed to have come to little. Nevertheless the reputations of the modernist writers themselves continued to rise, and many influential critical books on Yeats, Eliot and Joyce appeared. The work of Harry Levin, Richard Ellmann and Hugh Kenner was influential, particularly in America, and the modernist writers became the fashionable quarry for research. But other scholars, following Winters, began to criticize the modernist movement itself. Frank Kermode's *Romantic Image* (1957) argued that the idea of a dissociation of sensibility was a misleading myth shoring up the Romantic and modernist view that the Image was the central element in poetry, and suggested that 'discourse' too had an important part to play. C. K. Stead's *The New Poetic* (1964) discussed the work of Yeats and Eliot in terms of Image and discourse, arguing that the poet who writes to make affirmations must use the latter, as Eliot did in his later *Four Quartets*.

Literary historians were thus beginning to see the development of the century in a new pattern. A. Alvarez in *The Shaping Spirit* (1958) argued that 'Modernism ... has been predominantly an American concern', because it was the American poets who needed to establish a poetic manner. English poets like Lawrence and Auden, it was suggested, were not so systematic. A similar view was presented by Graham Hough in *Image and Experience* (1960). In 'The Nature of a Revolution' Hough discussed the movement as 'a cosmopolitan affair', rootless in its lack of an assured audience: 'Many of the great works of modern literature seem to exist in a vacuum, to spring from no particular society and to address no particular audience.' Most modernist writers would accept this description, but be more doubtful than Hough seems to be about possible alternatives. He went on to argue that the revolution had been 'one of technique and sensibility, not a movement of the spirit in any profound sense.' The main gain was Eliot's improvement of

poetic diction, providing 'a set of admirable tools' for the contemporary poet. But the case of Hardy as a poet suggests that these
improvements were of limited importance: 'Without the aid of
fertility rituals or the collective unconscious, he has shown how the
provincial can become the universal.' This more directly human
approach to literature is presented as characteristically English, and
a possible source of vitality for the future.

Other critics were, however, defending the achievement of the
modernists. Stephen Spender, originally one of the 'political' poets
of the 1930s, paid his tribute to 'the great experimenters in writing
at the beginning of the century' in *The Creative Element* (1953). He
saw a movement back towards various forms of orthodoxy in later
writers, and felt the dangers of this to the autonomous imagination.
'The literature of individualist vision' was considered in Baudelaire,
Rimbaud, and especially Rilke, whose poems Spender translated.
Although he noted the danger of excess – 'a serious mistake of
writers like Joyce, Proust and Rilke has been to attempt too much
transformation' and so eliminate the challenging 'otherness' of the
universe – Spender's sympathy was clearly with these writers.
Eliot's *Four Quartets* are said to lack life because of their reliance
on an external philosophy to provide a pattern, whereas Rilke's
*Duino Elegies* are 'densely populated with humanity' and constitute
'perhaps the last major achievement of a movement that has already
passed into history.' A similar historical view may be discerned in
other writings of this time, though tones and attitudes vary.

A polemical assertion was made by Harry Levin in a lecture of
1960 entitled 'What was Modernism?', printed in *Refractions*
(1966). In his introductory note to this lecture for the book, Levin
insisted that the process of decline from the achievement of the
modernists was continuing:

Yet Beckett, after Joyce, seems thin and strident and monoton-
ous, Miller looks like an amusing but crude burlesque of
Lawrence. The catcall, Who's Afraid of Virginia Woolf, lends
voice to an insecure bravado; contrivers of shoddy effects, like

Edward Albee, have reason to be afraid of Virginia Woolf.

There seemed nothing but 'a chorus of whimpers' to shield humanity from the impending bang. In the Preface to *Beyond Culture* (1966) Lionel Trilling, in his more restrained way, seemed to have become sceptical of the unquestioned social value of modernist art, writing of its need to be subject to 'the scrutiny of the rational intellect'. And in a final essay on 'The Two Environments: Reflections on the Study of English', he associated himself with Saul Bellow's recently expressed view that the pessimistic modernist view of the world had dwindled into a cliché, going so far as to recall Keats' view that poetry is less than all-important, just as 'an eagle is not so fine a thing as a truth'. For his doubts Trilling was taken to task by Harry Levin in his introductory note to 'What Was Modernism?' Levin argued that the modernists had identified the forces of unreason, but more recent writers had surrendered to them with their emphasis on spontaneity and 'happenings'. (It had been Winters' argument that Eliot had surrendered to unreason.)

Stephen Spender advanced his discussion of these issues in *The Struggle of the Modern* (1963). In this distinguished and far-ranging book Spender defined modern art convincingly as 'that in which the artist reflects awareness of an unprecedented modern situation in its form and idiom.' He contrasted this with the art which concerns itself with current issues in a more directly journalistic way, like that of Shaw or Wells, whom he described as 'contemporary' writers. Although the distinction is valid, this usage seems too awkward to survive. Spender noted the elements of hatred and nostalgia in the modernists, arguing that their works were held together not by 'a philosophy or a belief but some all-including emotional attitude towards the present – hope, hatred, despair.' Looking primarily at the recent literature of England, Spender drew a contrast which, though less dramatic than that drawn by Levin, was equally clear as to the superiority of the modernist achievement. He concluded:

Perhaps a deliberate, conscious, limited, cautious poetry of experiences, carefully chosen and rationally explored, is inevitable today. But the works of the modern movement stand behind us not only by reason of their being so much more ambitious but because they wrestle with the universal predicament which is still our world.

Recent criticism has therefore come to see Modernism as a highly significant form of art, attempting to render the depths of modern experience in an appropriate form, but it has been sensibly eclectic in its preparedness to accept other approaches too. Marxist reservations about Modernism were clearly expressed by David Craig in his essay 'Loneliness and Anarchy: Aspects of Modernism' in *The Real Foundations* (1973). While the committed writer grapples with 'the forces of disruption', the modernist is likely 'to conceive disorder as the absurdly random, cruelly inexplicable condition of existence that has him trapped.' But although he makes these distinctions, Craig is eclectic enough to suggest that literature is likely to develop along three main lines – one from realism, one from the oral culture of the working class, and one from modernism, which he recognizes in the work of Beckett and Pinter. And in this eclecticism he is joined by other critics of quite different persuasions and approaches. David Lodge ended *The Novelist at the Crossroads* (1971) with 'a modest affirmation of faith in the future of realistic fiction' alongside the 'products of the apocalyptic imagination'. And Malcolm Bradbury asserted in 'The Making of the Modern Tradition' in *The Social Context of Modern English Literature* (1971) that readers still find intelligible narrative 'a recurrent pleasure'. Modernism, that is to say, has not supplanted other ways of experiencing the world, nor other forms of art. A comparable point of view may be discerned in the conclusion to Michael Hamburger's *The Truth of Poetry* (1969), where he talks of the paradoxical relationship between beauty and truth, fiction and reality. Modernism was one ambitious and partly successful attempt to cope with this paradox: in its great works, the fictions are intensely human. Modernism has thus permanently enriched our literature, though leaving its problems unresolved. It has sharpened and intensified our awareness of the complexity of existence and so our need of, what it suggests we cannot have, a unifying philosophy.

There have therefore been a number of important developments since about 1930, both in the arts themselves and in critical attitudes. The more directly political art which emerged in the Thirties has been continued in various forms of social realism, though the example of Brecht shows that social criticism can be conveyed by expressionist or modernist methods. Modernism has come to seem a broadly homogeneous movement, with roots in Romanticism and a flowering in the first third of this century. This recognition of it has been accompanied by some stringent criticisms, especially from Marxist critics like Lukács and Craig, and from critics with a particular view of the English creative tradition, like Hough and Davie. At the same time Modernism has been vigorously defended, particularly in America and France. New forms of experimentation have developed, particularly since 1950, in the works of Beckett, Burroughs, Borges, Butor, Robbe-Grillet, in forms of concrete poetry and electronic music, in the mixing of media and the increasing application of sophisticated technology in music and the graphic arts. These developments raise questions of terminology. Is all this to be seen and described as an extension and continuation of Modernism, or is it a new movement which needs a new name?

We are in fact too closely involved in the situation to be able to answer these questions definitely, but it may be suggested that the recent innovations are not enough to constitute a new movement in the arts equivalent to Modernism in the early part of the century. There is justification for Frank Kermode's suggestion in 'The Discrimination of Modernism' in *Continuities* (1968) that it makes sense to see the art of Duchamp, Cage, Tinguely, Rauschenberg and Burroughs as a second phase of Modernism: 'there has been only one Modernist Revolution, and it happened a long time ago'. Kermode therefore suggested the use of the terms 'palaeo-modernism' and 'neo-modernism'. Bernard Bergonzi accepted this usage in his Introduction to *Innovations* (1968), preferring neo-modernist to 'avant-garde'. But whatever description is finally arrived at for the art that has emerged *since* Eliot and Pound, Joyce and Virginia Woolf, there can be little doubt that *their* achievement was both substantial enough and similar enough in spirit and methods to justify the term Modernism itself. It is perhaps the high seriousness of their devotion to art which finally distinguishes the modernists from their successors, who set more store by jokes and language-games. That very intelligent and sensitive writer B. S. Johnson concluded *Christie Malry's Own Double Entry* in 1973 with a scene in which the author visits his character Christie in hospital, dying of cancer. Christie reproaches his creator:

> 'In any case', he said, almost to himself, not looking at me, 'you shouldn't be writing bloody novels about it, you should be out there bloody doing something about it.'
>
> And the nurses then suggested that I should leave, not knowing who I was, that he could not die without me.

For the modernists, however, there was no such scepticism about art, the one value they adhered to with total devotion in a universe which they knew and showed to be bewilderingly problematic.

# Bibliography

*Relevant Writers*

In order to limit the size of this bibliography, it has been restricted to critical writings by the relevant writers. For a fuller record of their work students should consult *The Cambridge Bibliography of English Literature*, Vol IV, ed. I. R. Willison, Cambridge, 1972.

Fore-runners

James, Henry, A good selection is available entitled *Henry James: Selected Literary Criticism*, ed. Morris Shapira, London, 1963.
James, Henry, *The Art of the Novel*, ed. R. P. Blackmur, New York, 1934.
    Consists of James's Prefaces to the New York Edition of his works, with a useful introductory essay.
Yeats, William Butler, *Essays and Introductions*, London and New York, 1961.
    Includes most of the important criticism.

The modernists

This list has been restricted to the central Anglo-American figures.

Eliot, Thomas Stearns, *Selected Essays*, London, 1951.
    Contains the earlier essays Eliot himself selected.
Joyce, James, *The Critical Writings of James Joyce*, ed. E. Mason and R. Ellmann, London, 1959. A small volume; Joyce differed from most other modernists in writing little criticism.

Lawrence, David Herbert, *Selected Literary Criticism*, ed. A. Beal, London, 1956. Important evidence for considering the question of Lawrence's Modernism.

Pound, Ezra, *Literary Essays of Ezra Pound*, ed. T. S. Eliot, London, 1954. A lively selection from all but the first and last of Pound's volumes of criticism.

Woolf, Virginia, *Collected Essays*, 4 vols, London, 1966.

Other relevant writers

It is impossible to specify all the writers who are relevant, but this list includes major American and European writers: Ford, Ford Madox; Lewis, Wyndham; Crane, Hart; Faulkner, William; Stevens, Wallace; Williams, William Carlos; Kafka, Franz; Mann, Thomas; Mayakovsky, Vladimir; Proust, Marcel; Rilke, Rainer Maria.

*General and background studies*

No comments are made on books discussed in the text.

The rise of modernism

Beckett, Samuel, *Proust*, London, 1931. A subtle essay, interesting for its subject and its author.

Empson, William, *Seven Types of Ambiguity*, London, 1930. A brilliant discussion of types of poetic complexity.

Forster, Edwin Morgan, *Aspects of the Novel*, London, 1927. A typically urbane and balanced discussion.

Graves, Robert and Riding, Laura, *A Survey of Modernist Poetry*, London, 1927.

Hulme, Thomas Ernest, *Speculations*, London, 1924. An important assertion of anti-Romantic ideas, admired by Eliot.

Leavis, Frank Raymond, *New Bearings in English Poetry*, London, 1932.

Leavis, Frank Raymond, *Revaluation*, London, 1936.
  Applies a modernist critical approach to the English poetic
  tradition.
Lewis, Wyndham, *Blasting and Bombardiering*, London, 1937.
  An autobiographical memoir of 'the men of 1914'.
Lubbock, Percy, *The Craft of Fiction*, London, 1921. Stresses the
  Jamesian achievement of impersonality.
Read, Herbert, *Form in Modern Poetry*, London, 1932.
Richards, I. A. *The Principles of Literary Criticism*, London, 1924.
Wilson, Edmund, *Axël's Castle*, New York, 1931.


Historical discussions

Alvarez, A., *The Shaping Spirit*, London, 1958.
Auerbach, E., *Mimesis: The Representation of Reality in Western
  Literature*, 1946, translated by R. Trask, Princeton, 1971.
  Ch. 20 'The Brown Stocking' discusses Mrs Ramsay in *To the
  Lighthouse*.
Bergonzi, Bernard, 'The Advent of Modernism' in *The Sphere of
  History of Literature in the English Language*, Vol VII, *The
  Twentieth Century*; other relevant articles are 'The Novel in the
  1920's' by Malcolm Bradbury, and 'Literary Criticism in Eng-
  land in the Twentieth Century' by David Lodge.
Bowra, Maurice, *The Creative Experiment*, London, 1949. Ranges
  widely to include Cavafy, Apollinaire, Mayakovsky, Eliot, Lorca
  and Alberti.
Bradbury, Malcolm, *The Social Context of Modern English Litera-
  ture*, London, 1971.
  An interesting discussion of the relation of Modernism in the arts
  to the modernization of society.
Bradbury, Malcolm, *Possibilities*, London, 1973. Includes a section
  of four thoughtful essays on 'Modernisms'.
Brooks, Cleanth, *Modern Poetry and the Tradition*, New York, 1948.
  Insists on the importance of irony and paradox in poetry.
Craig, David, *The Real Foundations*, London, 1973.

Daiches, David, *The Novel and the Modern World*, London, 1938; revised edition, 1960.

Daiches, David, *Poetry and the Modern World*, New York, 1940.

Davie, Donald, *Purity of Diction in English Verse*, London, 1952.

Davie, Donald, *Articulate Energy. An Enquiry into the Syntax of English Poetry*, London, 1955.

Davie, Donald, *Thomas Hardy and British Poetry*, London, 1973.

Donoghue, Denis, *The Ordinary Universe*, London, 1968.

Ellmann, Richard, *Yeats, The Man and the Masks*, London, 1949.

Ellmann, Richard, *The Identity of Yeats*, London, 1954.

Ellmann, Richard, *James Joyce*, London, 1959.

and Fiedelson, Charles, *The Modern Tradition. Backgrounds of Modern Literature*, New York, 1965.

An extensive anthology of material from the late-eighteenth to the mid-twentieth century.

Fraser, George S., *The Modern Writer and His World*, London, 1953; revised edition, 1964.

Hamburger, Michael, *The Truth of Poetry*, London, 1969.

A far-ranging discussion from Baudelaire to the 1960s.

Hough, Graham, *Image and Experience. Studies in a Literary Revolution*, London, 1960.

Kenner, Hugh, *The Poetry of Ezra Pound*, New York, 1951.

Kenner, Hugh, *Gnomon*, New York, 1958.

Kenner, Hugh, *The Invisible Poet: T. S. Eliot*, London and New York, 1960.

Kenner, Hugh, *Samuel Beckett*, New York, 1961.

Kenner, Hugh, *The Stoic Comedians*, New York, 1964.

Kenner, Hugh, *The Pound Era*, New York, 1971.

One of the most active and committed critics concerned with Modernism.

Kermode, Frank, *Romantic Image*, London, 1957.

Kermode, Frank, *The Sense of an Ending*, London, 1967.

Discusses the apocalyptic vision in modern literature.

Kermode, Frank, *Continuities*, London, 1968.

Includes a consideration of types of Modernism.

Levin, Harry, *James Joyce. A Critical Introduction*, New York, 1944; revised edition, 1960.

Levin, Harry, *Refractions*, New York, 1966.
Includes the lecture 'What was Modernism?' of 1960.

Lukács, Georg, *The Meaning of Contemporary Realism*, 1937; translated by J. and N. Mander, London, 1963.

Miller, J. Hillis, *Poets of Reality*, New York, 1966.
A suggestive account of Conrad, Yeats, Eliot, Stevens, Williams and Dylan Thomas.

Sartre, Jean-Paul, *What is Literature?*, translated by B. Frechtman, New York, 1949.
An existentialist approach to many central questions.

Spender, Stephen, *The Creative Element*, London, 1953.

Spender, Stephen, *The Struggle of the Modern*, London, 1963.

Stallman, R. W. (ed.), *Critiques and Essays in Criticism 1920–1948*, New York, 1949.
Includes Joseph Frank's article 'Spatial Form in Modern Literature'.

Stead, C. K., *The New Poetic*, London, 1964.
An incisive account of 'image' and 'discourse' in Yeats and Eliot.

Winters, Yvor, *In Defence of Reason*, New York, 1947.

Recent developments

Barthes, Roland, *Writing Degree Zero*, translated by Annette Lavers and Colin Smith, London, 1967.
An important essay based on a structuralist approach to literature.

Bergonzi, Bernard (ed.), *Innovations, Essays in Art and Ideas*, London, 1968.
A varied collection of essays on aspects of recent culture.

Borges, Jorge Luis, *Other Inquisitions 1927–1952*, translated by Ruth Simms, Austin, Texas, 1964. Representative articles by a major formal innovator.

Butor, Michel, *Inventory*, translated by Richard Howard, London, 1970.

A challenging work by an important French novelist and theorist.

Josipovici, Gabriel, *The World and the Book*, London, 1971.

A difficult book attempting to formulate a general theory of modern literature.

Kostelanetz, Richard (ed.), *On Contemporary Literature*, New York, 1964.

An introductory essay discusses the relation of contemporary writers to their modernist predecessors.

Robbe-Grillet, Alain, *Snapshots and Towards a New Novel*, translated by Barbara Wright, London, 1965.

Gives the theory underlying the author's radical innovations.

Sontag, Susan, *Against Interpretation and Other Essays*, London, 1967.

Stimulating advocacy of a 'non-judging' approach to art.

# Index